THE GOLD THREAD

The Cantos of Ezra Pound and other works by Pound listed in this book's bibliography—*ABC of Economics; Collected Early Poems; The Guide to Kulchur; Impact; Gold and Work; Literary Essays of Ezra Pound; Selected Poems; Translations of Ezra Pound; A Visiting Card*—are quoted by permission of Faber & Faber, London.

British Library Cataloguing-in-Publication Data: A catalogue record for this book is available from the British Library.

Published by: Diwan Press
                 311 Allerton Road
                 Bradford
                 BD15 7HA
                 UK
Website: www.diwanpress.com
E-mail: info@diwanpress.com

Paperback ISBN 978-1-914397-39-4

THE GOLD THREAD

Ezra Pound's Principles
of
Good Government
& Sound Money

by Robert Luongo

DIWAN PRESS
FOUNDED IN 1975

Acknowledgments

I would like to mention James Laughlin, to whom we owe so much of the preservation of Pound's work-in-print today. Laughlin's efforts as a student, editor and friend of Mr. Pound provided him with a lifelong commitment to see Ezra Pound's writing made available.

C. F. Terrell and Hugh Kenner are singled out for their serious and in-depth scholarship in the field of Pound studies.

My thanks to Matthew Flynn at University College, London, for his help in the early stages of the book.

I would like to thank Abdassamad Clark of Norwich, England and Rick Feher of Northern California, two talented and exceedingly patient proof readers and editors, for their help in preparing the manuscript for print.

Credit is due to Dr. Abd al-Alim Palmer for his assistance with the etymology of the Chinese characters.

Appropriately left to last, as the single most important influence and aid in my own life's journey, is Shaykh Abdalqadir Al-Murabit, whom I thank for his pre-eminent contribution toward my accomplishing this study of Pound.

Contents

I

To Make a Tapestry

A warrior poet of the twentieth century, not unlike the ancient heroes of his Odyssean epic, *The Cantos,* Ezra Pound wore the mantel of Teutonic activism into a battle that spanned more than fifty years of his life. He was a volitionist visionary who strove to realize his *ideas in action.* Through the long circumnavigation of his unfolding Odyssey, constructed along the lines of a musical score rather than a sequential narrative, it was his quest to see a just and enlightened system of governance. Good government, he believed, must first establish a clear and precise definition of words, hence the importance of language. Upon doing this, leadership must create a healthy and clean monetary system that puts wealth (and credit) into the hands of people, not an oligarchic élite who would (assuredly!) build a pernicious, and, in

Pound's view, filthy system that would see all nation-states reduced to debt receptors, all culture, art, and religions destroyed and the vast majority of the world's population *debased* into a citizenry of debtor-slaves. It should be seen, right from the very start, that while Pound was revered as "the last American living the tragedy of Europe," it was nothing less than the pre-cipitant destruction of European civilization that he was trying to avert. (James E. Miller's *The American Quest for a Supreme Fiction.*)

While the *magnum opus* of Pound's literary career is undisputedly *The Cantos*, his prose writing, which took the form of historical and educational essays as well as full-length texts, make up an essential part of his work. A great deal of what appears in *The Cantos*, particularly in relation to his monetary principles, ideas of good govern-ment and social and cultural elevation, are the subject matters of those prose pieces. Other significant areas of Pound's endeavors were his literary criticisms, prin-cipally those on the works of his friends—T. S. Eliot, Wyndham Lewis, Ernest Hemingway, William Carlos Williams, Gaudier-Brzeska, James Joyce and Hilda Doolittle (H. D.)—for whom he was a tireless champion and supporter. There were also his translations which included the three main books by Confucius, the *Confucian Odes* (for which Confucius was the anthologist and collector), early Anglo-Saxon verse and selected poems from his much-loved Provençal troubadour bards. All of these various strains found their way back into the weave of his great musical tapestry, the *Cantos*. It is here that the words of the distinguished Pound critic, Hugh Kenner, from his serious work, *The Pound Era,* set the stage for what is to be the theme of my own work. Kenner says, "These ideas of wealth [money created as interest debt, artificial scarcities, monopolies...] are not extrinsic to the *Cantos*, but warp and woof." To elaborate on Kenner's succinct statement it is recognizable that in the same *ideogrammatic* manner, used by Pound in creating *meaning-forms* ("a radiant node or cluster, a Vortex...from which and through which and into which ideas are constantly rushing." —*Selected Essays*) that what functions as warp and woof on the one level becomes totally expressed as design on another. These principles, then, are displayed in much the same manner that one would see expansive winged trusses in a vaulted cathedral ceiling or support beams in traditional Japanese house construction.

The slew of pseudo-scholarship, throwing up statements like, "a flawed genius who strayed into incoherent and obtuse theories about economics, government and history..." reveals how far the censorship of his work has been taken. Censorship, in this case, taking the form of covering-up by the act of obscuring, and discrediting, the man and his ideas under a heaped up mountain of wastepaper. This, of course, is exactly what has been done to Richard Wagner by the tantrum-throwing highchair academics who have built their careers on infantile slander and *ressentement*. (See Nietzsche's *Genealogy of Morals*.) Yet, when all is said and done, the rapturously beautiful music dramas of Wagner have never ceased thrilling the hearts and minds of those who are capable of listening. Likewise, despite all of the insipid attacks on the poet and obfuscation of his work, those tepid snifflers have not been able to put Pound—the man and his masterpiece—to rest.

II

Current Curriculum

THE COURSE to be charted begins with Confucius, whom Pound insisted was as relevant today, as in the fifth century B.C. According to Pound this is true of the study of classical Greek Literature; the glory of Rome; the Italian Renaissance; the later half of eighteenth-century America (with the advent of Jefferson, Adams, and Van Buren and their prodigious attempt to create "honest bills of exchange" with "no interest on them," says Adams); 1829 to 1841 and Andy Jackson's war from the White House against the banks [Jackson defeated the renewal of the First National Bank's charter which, despite its official sounding name, was a privately owned company with the monopoly rights to lend (rent) credit to the Nation]; the 1860s through the 1890s and the decline of American civilization in the aftermath of the Civil War. Pound tells us that the turning point of that civilization was the passing of the National Banking Act, a bill passed through the American Congress, sponsored by Ohio Congressman John Sherman, lobbied into law by its original designers, the English bankers, the Rothschild Brothers with the collaboration of the Wall Street firm of Iklesheimer, Morton and Vandergould. "Any nation that pays rent for its credit are fools," said a Mr. Rothschild to Disraeli, then Prime Minister of England. The list continues with the events taking place in Europe during what Pound called the "century of Usurocracy," followed by World War I which brought about the final destruction of all of Europe's ruling monarchies as well as the Islamic Caliphate. Last on his list was the difficult task of coming to grips with, and making sense of, the deafening crescendo of the Second World War.

What Pound believed to be within the *relevant* scope of essential knowledge and understanding of history remains a prodigious challenge for any serious person. That some people of action should understand his work in order to make a world lit by the lamp of our "cultural heritage," (*Impact*, Essays by Ezra Pound) stands forth in sharp contrast against the hollow goals of a consumed society. Pound had said that it was "rash to write an epic in a time of chaos," yet that was precisely what he did. Since the aftermath of the Second World War the world had remained frozen in a cold war stasis, only to arrive thawed before the *terrifying* promise (mutant offspring of

the French Revolution) of a one world state, totally in the
control of a non-elected usurious oligarchy.

   This view of history, which Pound relentlessly put
forth as crucial for the true education of people so as not
to be "duped" by the mercantilism of modern publishing
houses,

> And the betrayers of language
> . . . . .n and the press gang
> And those who had lied for hire;
> the perverts, the perverters of language,
>   the perverts, who have set money-lust
> Before the pleasures of the senses;

> howling, as of a hen-yard in a printing house,

                    Canto XIV

is best described by Clark Emery in *Ideas into Action*.
Emery relates, "In his study of history, the effort will be to
recapture the intensity of life being lived, and, instead of
bringing history to the reader to bring the reader into
history. That is, the reader will not witness an event as an
accomplished fact, but will seem to be a participant in the
event. He will, therefore, often receive fragmentary
information, thus being [momentarily] as confused or
ignorant or misled as the original actors. He will often

have to speak the language of the time, the dialect of the place. On the other hand, though pressed into action, he will simultaneously maintain his perspective as reader and will be able to draw inferences [and important insights] from startling juxtapositions or apparently divergent times, persons, places, events, ideas."

While the entirety of Cantos XLIV and XLVI provide excellent examples of "bringing the reader into the events" (as do nearly all the *Cantos*), I have chosen to excerpt just a handful of lines in illustration. The first phrase may be heard as an official declaration on behalf of the Grand Duke, sounded in the city square.

ND thou shalt not, Firenze 1766, and thou shalt not
sequestrate for debt any farm implement
nor any yoke ox nor
any peasant while he works with the same
                    Pietro Leopaldo

                                        Canto XLIV

Ferdinando EVVIVA!!
                    declared against exportation
thought grain was to eat.

Flags trumpets horns drums
and a placard

VIVA FERDINANDO
and were sounded all carillons
with bombs and with bonfires and was sung TE·DEUM
in thanks to the Highest for this so
provident law

Canto XLIV

'The foundation, Siena, has been to keep bridle on
usury.'

Nicolò Piccolomini, Provveditore.

Canto XLIV

The following passage, now from Canto XLVI, takes
up a dialogue constructed by Pound from conversations
he had with Marmaduke Pickthall, an English *journalist*
and orientalist concerning the behaviour of the British
government in the near east. There is a previous reference
in the poem to Balfour, the British statesman who drafted
the famous "agreement" of the same name that gave up
Palestine. Another reference, found in the following line,
mentions 'ole Johnny Bull with an "ankerchief," which
evokes the British archetype and their two-faced dealings
with the desert Arabs, particularly the mad masquerad-
ing Lawrence, who, after gaining the trust of his hosts,
sold them out. This indicates that Pound wanted to bring
both examples to mind.

"Englishman goes there, lives honest, word is reliable,
"ten years, they believe him, then he signs terms for his
                                                government.
  "and, naturally, the treaty is broken, Mohammedans,
"Nomads, will never understand how we do this."
17 years on this case, and we not the first lot!

Canto XLVI proceeds with a statement by William
Paterson who founded the Bank of England in 1694. This
is followed by a bit of biting dialogue with one speaker
addressing us from the mid 1860s, and the other from the
early 1930s. The first speaker, a Mr. Rothschild, whose
family was then, and still is today, one of the most
powerful banking families in the world. The Rothschild
name, throughout the *Cantos*, creatively takes on the
poetically-charged meaning of *usurers personified*. The
second voice circa 1930s would be the poet himself.

Said Paterson:
                Hath benefit of interest on all
the moneys which it, the bank, creates out of nothing.

        Semi-private inducement
Said Mr RothSchild, hell knows which Roth-schild
1861, '64 or there sometime, "Very few people
"will understand this. Those who do will be occupied

"getting profits. The general public will probably not
"see it's against their interest."
        Seventeen years on the case; here   ·
Gents, is/are the confessions.
        "Can we take this into court?
        "Will any jury convict on this evidence?

The Canto, as it draws towards its end, building in
intensity reads:

Aurum est commune sepulchrum. Usura, commune sepulchrum.
helandros   kai heleptolis   kai helarxe.
Hic Geryon est. Hic hyperusura.

                                Canto XLVI

[Gold is a common sepulcher. Usury, a common
sepulcher, destroyer of men, and destroyer of cities, and
destroyer of governments.]
["Here is Geryon. Here is hyper usury."]

    Geryon was a three-headed monster living on the
island of Erythia, killed by Heracles. In his *Inferno*, Dante
used Geryon as both the symbol of fraud and for guard-
ing of the eighth circle of hell, as well as the symbol of
usury and violence against nature and art.

FIVE million youths without jobs
FOUR million adult illiterates
15 million 'vocational misfits', that is with small chance for jobs
Nine million persons annual, injured in preventable industrial
                                            accidents
One hundred thousand violent crimes. The Eunited States ov
                                            America
3rd year of the reign of F. Roosevelt, signed F. Delano, his uncle.
CASE for the prosecution. That is one case, minor case
in the series/ Eunited States of America, a.d. 1935
England a worse case, France under a foetor of regents.
'Mr. Cummings wants Farley's job headline in current paper.

Canto XLVI

Pound gives us here in staccato rapid-fire some current statistics of his day. We hear them with the memory still fresh in our minds of those "so provident laws" of Pietro Leopaldo which would be the safeguard against such atrocities. The last line being a bit of newspaper fodder which provides its own irony: Mr. Cummings, an American lawyer and one-time U.S. Attorney General wants Mr. Farley's job, which we learn was the lucrative post of United States Postmaster, given him as a *political favor*. (See C. Terrell's *Companion to the Cantos*.)

A basic understanding of Pound's way of viewing history together with his method of constructing his epic and the various uses of styles and meters will accompany us in the perusal of his ideas on governance and money. The stressed significance of the "necessity of the clear definition of words"—taken from the *TaHio* of Confucius, rubbed in later on by Dante, picked up on by Ford Maddox Ford (an early literary mentor of Pound), will resound its message in our inner ear. The discovery of Major C. H. Douglas, the twentieth-century British engineer turned monetary reformer, and his theory on the increment of association "and the incredulity of total costs (of production) in their (falsified) relation to purchasing power" bring up important questions. Likewise, can we follow the *traces* of the hard-fought battles of Jefferson, Adams and Martin Van Buren against the impossibility of creating a just State without establishing a just money?

These questions and more, which bring us to the post-World-War-II period, were ones that Pound continued to put forth and elucidate up until 1969. Although Pound's personal odyssey came to an end in 1972, it did not in any way bring to an end the imperatives of his immense battle. *The Cantos* stand full of splendor, lucidity, intricacies and words 言 by which man 人 stands: A man standing by his words—

"integrity." As we enter into the closing years of this century, with so much of what Pound fought to preserve and restore: the preservation of languages and cultures, the importance of the rituals and acts of worship of the Divine, the necessity of an honest means of exchange to facilitate the natural intercourse of trading goods and services, and a form of governance that can stand firmly to safeguard each of these, now threatened and endangered to the point of extinction, we must take seriously the lessons of this committed genius. The eye seeks its aim.

> And he said
>   "Anyone can run to excesses,
> It is easy to shoot past the mark,
> It is hard to stand firm in the middle."

Canto XIII

There are, undoubtedly, esteemed academics who are dying of embarrassment at the very thought of Pound not running to excesses. They have, unfortunately, taken their detached objectivism as a substitute for passion and the ability to derive meaning from what they study. Pound, on the other hand, never lacked for either.

While the poet suffered greatly from both physical and mental exhaustion during his cruel imprisonment in

Pisa at an American concentration camp, he was, nevertheless, able to reflect on both what was happening to him as an individual and also to the civilization of which he was a part. No further proof of this is needed other than the *Pisan Cantos,* which he wrote during that time. That collection stands firmly as one of the greatest pieces of verse written in the English language and is a hallmark of twentieth-century literature. Pound was awarded, much to the deep embarrassment of the U.S. Government, the prestigious Bollingen Prize (sponsored through the U.S. Library of Congress) for the *Pisan Cantos* for the highest accomplishment of poetry in the year 1949.

All the same, the long thirteen years he spent locked up in St. Elizabeth's Hospital in Washington D.C. virtually *sentenced for life* (to a mad-house) for a crime he was never tried for, added to the immense strain put upon him. If he was a mad poet, why didn't they leave him wandering in the hillsides of his *imaginary* Italy? (*Vision Fugitive* by E. Davies.) If he was a traitor, why was he not tried and shot? Tragically, Ezra Pound was punished for what he wrote and spoke.

III

Kung

To MAKE A CLEAR exposition of Pound's theories, we are to begin with the Master Kung. Whether as Kung futz-æ (the phonetic transliteration of the Chinese sage's name) or Confucius, we can be certain that the master's identity emerges as much from Pound's discoveries of the historical manuscripts available when he wrote, followed then by his own crafted translations of the ancient Chinese texts, as it did from his own lifelong pursuit to make *it* all cohere. Pound understood the necessity for cohesion as regards a man, his ideas and his actions as a pure *Confucian act*. The reference to Pound's struggle for *cohesion* comes from Canto CXVI, written between 1958-59 when he was 74, at the time of his release from St. Elizabeth's (18th April 1958) with the indictment of treason dropped. Thereby, we have a fifty year cycle of character development since Pound first began to write on Confucius in the early 1900s. Pound's translations of the main body of Confucius's work have held up to be considered among the best available. He gives us his "gist," often using an unpretentious rural colloquial voice that sticks to the point far better than any of the earlier enigmatic translations of the ideograms that appeared *en français* or in the laborious parlour language of the late nineteenth-century British orientalists.

Pound began his work from notes on the Chinese characters, made by Ernest Fenollosa while living in Japan, which Pound received as a gift from Fenellosa's widow. Pound said of *The Great Digest (TaHio)*, *The Unwobbling Pivot (Chung-Yung)*, and *The Analects*, that they were "my most important work, though few would realize." His reading of Confucius goes from *what did Confucius say*—constructed from a literal transposing of the characters into English words—to *what did he mean*. Exacting philology inevitably gives way to clear perceptions registered on the heart.

Having, so far, introduced Kung-futz-æ as both historical and literary figure we come to the primary Confucian answer from the Master when asked about the *first act of government*: "Call things by their right names," (precise verbal definitions).

A century later, Mencius reverberated the same message, confirming Pound's conviction that all men concerned with truth will be in agreement with each other, "two ends of the same tally-stick"—a Confucian theme that Pound will teach us can span centuries, cultures and continents.

The importance of the word, the clear definition of terms as something commonly understood and known, together with men capable and committed to stand by them, is what can be noted as Pound's first lesson on Confucius. What follows is from Pound's translation of the master.

> Tze Lu: The Lord Wei is waiting for you to form a government, what are you going to do first?
> Kung: Settle the names (determine a precise terminology)
> Tze-Lu: How's this, you're divagating, why fix 'em?
> Kung: You bumkin! Sprout! When a proper man don't know a thing, he shows some reserve. If words (terminology) are not (is not) precise, they cannot be followed out, or completed in action according to specifications.

Pound wasted no time in getting down to business in saying that one of the most important words that people of any given society need to know the meaning of is money. The next Confucian principle, therefore, is needed: "The creation of a just state must be established on a just means of exchange." Hence, without understanding what money is "and also isn't, folks will be duped" and able to be exploited. According to Pound, both Mill, the capitalist theorist, and Marx had it wrong. Marx: "commodities in so far as they are values, are materialized labor." Mill hardly differs as he defined capital as, "the accumulated stock of human labor." Both men falsify the word as they define money as an accumulation of energy. Both statements "deny both God and nature." Consequently, when Stalin speaks of "disposing" of forty truck-loads of human "material" for work on a canal, no liberal from any *free market economy* could object as they too are always on about the "export of labor." Of course, our liberals would balk at the mention of Stalin's name, while being unable to demonstrate any fundamental difference in their contempt for the human personality. Liberalism conceals its pernicious economics under the two false pretexts of "the freedom of the spoken and written word, protected, in theory, by trial in open court." (*The Enemy is Ignorance*, Pound.)

With the fact that liberals form the bastion of nearly all Western universities, universities that rest on the support of centrist state government policies and usurious business backing, it is a wonder that so few people have found this extremely odd. Pound identifies liberalism and Bolshevism as being in intimate agreement. The next step is to recognize how liberal academics have been able to redefine man according to their *idealism* (born out of *ideals* from the French Revolution). At the end of the day, you have produced millions of free-thinking people, popping off the conveyor belt of a modern university education, who become the unqualified supporters and bulwark for the privileged private interests of an élite of financiers and bankers, whom, by all standards of their dialectical diatribe, they would seem to oppose. The newly educated masses are equally convinced that the thrust of free market economy, advertising and media programming, offers them what they as individuals really want, as they are also convinced that a bank's privileges to "earn interest on money which it [the bank] creates out of nothing" is a normal and necessary practice. Pound keeps hounding us to heed Confucius and "call things by their proper names." He also reserves some very choice names for both liberals and usurers.

The poet continues with his own clarification. Money "is an undated ticket that will be good when we want to use it. When we do not hand over money at once for goods or services received, we are said to have 'credit.' The 'credit' is the other man's belief that we can and will sometime hand over the money or something measured by money."

Aristotle, Pound relates, says of money, "It is a guarantee of future exchange." Money is not energy nor is it procreative. You cannot inseminate with it or plant it. Money is not a commodity and therefore not to be rented. It is a measure, an equal sign, between goods and/or services (in actual existence) and those that want or need them (Umar Vadillo's *End of Economics*). The fact that enough tickets should not exist within a given society when both resources and need exist is "downright" tyranny and injustice. Pound goes on to quote John Adams, the great American president, in Canto LXXI:

> Every bank of discount is downright corruption
> taxing the people for private individuals' gain.
>   and if I say this in my will
> the American people wd/ pronounce I died crazy.

The fact that John Adams and Thomas Jefferson, both Homeric heroes of the *Cantos*, helped pen the Constitution which stated that only "the Congress shall have power... to coin money [and] regulate the value thereof," an obvious fallacy in the history of America, reveals that the act of high treason was there from the very inception of the Nation. Ezra offers up Alexander Hamilton, and his strange foreign bed-fellows, as one historical example. Pound dates the decline of American Civilization from the passage of the National Banking Act at the end of the Civil War, where we can recall the cynical statement of the London banker, Rothschild (who played a major rôle in the passage of those U.S. banking laws), to the then Prime Minister of England: "Any nation that pays rent for its credit are fools." That money becomes a commodity thrown into speculative (manipulable) uncertainty is a perversion of its meaning and a means of "defrauding, sodomizing" and, according to both Aristotle and Cato, tantamount to murder. This abuse of money, this corrupting of the word, in its deepest Confucian sense, gives rise to usury.

Usury, as Pound defines it in a footnote to Canto XLV, "a charge for the use of purchasing power, levied without regard to production, sometimes without regard even to the possibilities of production," has oozed its way into the bloodstream of contemporary life. "Nothing," Pound states, "too disgusting can be said about them [usurers]." When the equal sign can change value, leaving people to pay double, triple or more than what they first received (paying back three bushels of wheat for the value of one) it becomes the most heinous crime, and our recent decades' proofs (Latin America, Africa and Asia) are heart-breaking examples. This is before we even get to the massive public and private debts of Western Europe and America, for which Thomas Jefferson's foreboding prophecy is all too ominous: "If the American people ever allow private banks to control the issue of their money, first by inflation, then by deflation, the banks and the corporations that will grow up around. them [stock exchanges, insurance companies] will deprive the people of their property until their children will wake up homeless on the continent their fathers conquered."

Mencius, the Confucian who lived 100 years after the Master, said, "None of our sages ever wanted or sought public office. They took it on as an obligation binding on them. When out of office, they returned to their original work of rectifying their hearts." Making a "scene-shift," a literary device or "trick" as Ezra called them, to show the correlatives in history (two ends of the tally stick) we hear the Prophet Muhammad, *peace and blessings be upon him*, when in the sixth century C.D. (Christian dating), he said, "Leadership is a responsibility binding on good men." When the Prophet was asked by a man of notable status if he, like others, could be sent to be a *wazir* (governor) to one of the various provinces outside of Madinah, he was told by the Prophet that "his wanting it disqualified him from having it."

Returning to an example from Pound's translation of the *TaHsio* of Confucius, a definitive clarification of the ageless wisdom follows.

"The men of old, wanting to clarify and diffuse
throughout the empire that light which comes
from looking straight into the heart and then
acting, first set up good government in their own
states; wanting good government in their states,
they first established order in their own families;

wanting order in the home, they first disciplined
themselves; desiring self-discipline, they rectified
their hearts and wanting to rectify their hearts,
they sought precise verbal definitions of their
inarticulate thoughts [the tones given off by the
heart]; wishing to attain precise verbal defini-
tions, they set out to extend their knowledge to
the utmost. This completion of knowledge is
rooted in sorting things into organic categories."

From Canto XIII, the famous Kung-Canto, Pound re-
enacts the scene, taken in part from translation as well as
his own "gist" of the meanings.

And "When the prince has gathered about him
"All the savants and artists, his riches will be fully employed."
And Kung said, and wrote on the bo leaves:
        If a man have not order within him
He can not spread order about him;
And if a man have not order within him
His family will not act with due order;
        And if the prince have not order within him
He can not put order in his dominions.
And Kung gave the words "order"
and "brotherly deference"
And said nothing of the "life after death."
And he said
        "Anyone can run to excesses,

It is easy to shoot past the mark,
It is hard to stand firm in the middle."

This Canto draws to its conclusion with the lines,

And Kung said, "Without character you will
    be unable to play on that instrument
Or to execute the music fit for the Odes.

The last lines, beautifully added by Pound,

The blossoms of the apricot
    blow from the east to the west,
And I have tried to keep them from falling."

This brief exposure to some of what Pound elicited
from the Chinese sage is our beginning and as Kung
plays an ongoing rôle throughout the *Cantos*, he does not
leave us in our effort. Before moving on, and to remind us
of its importance, I take an exchange of a few words
between Ezra and T. S. Eliot, to whom Pound often
referred, with the affectionate criticism of an old friend,
as "the Rev. Eliot." "And what does Mr. Pound believe?"
"I believe the *TaHio*." Thereby Pound's "need of
Confucius" indicates, "a lack, as a sick man has a need.
Something he has not. Kung as medicine?" (*Impact:
Immediate Need of Confucius*.)

The sickness of our age can be traced to the perversion of "money," culminating in the deaths of countless numbers, the devastation taking place in Brazil, Mexico and Somalia, along with the destruction of the very lungs of our planet, and millions of redundancies throughout countries like England, Scotland and Ireland, crippling not only local industry, but whole communities. This is all due to humanly and mathematically impossible national debts. We cannot pass lightly over what Pound stressed about the jargon of contemporary economists. Pound wrote, "There is a marasmus of books [on economics] that start, 'treating of this, that, or the other,' without defining their terminology, let alone their terms, or circle, of reference. A thousand infernal self-styled economists start off without even defining 'money' (which is a measured claim, transferable from anyone to anyone else, and which *does not bear interest.*) These unhandy writers then go on to muddle their readers with discussions of 'systems' of inflation; of cancellation; of credit problems. And naturally their work is useless and merely spreads ignorance."

The wasting away of the body, caused by an inadequate or unassimilable supply of food, what Pound explicated as a marasmus, is rhymed with the last two lines, in no uncertain and in strong language, of Canto XIV:

THE GOLD THREAD

monopolists, obstructors of knowledge,
obstructors of distribution.

Responsibility lies in looking from Pound's diagnosis (which was nothing less than his identification of USURA as the ROOT DISEASE) toward a prognosis that includes these past twenty years since his death in Venice, 1 November 1972.

With the proliferation of Economic Summits being held all over the world and the constant reshuffling of percentage points in relation to National Debts, GNPs versus devaluation, indexes and deficits running against import and export levels within an ever-changing Exchange Rate Mechanism, it is unlikely that Pound's prescriptions could be more valuable than now. The specifics of his remedies will be detailed further on in this study. They range from a bi-metal monetary system when availability is not devoured by MONOPOLY, to stamp-script, "social credit" and the creation of credit being based on

the abundance of nature
with the whole folk behind it.

Canto LII

which was typified for Pound by the Monte dei Paschi, "Mountain of Grazing Lands," founded as a beneficent institution in Siena, 1600. These models constitute the grist of Ezra Pound's ideas. While Pound's medicine and methods are those of true education together with the application of what he saw as the irrefutable wisdom of Confucius (and Kung-like men) we must look beyond the Hell Cantos of the nineteenth and first half of the twentieth century to conditions of today.

BROADCAST

The difficulty of perception in our time lies in the mesmerizing effect of a screen that has been erected to absorb any incisive understanding of how whole nations have been robbed in broad daylight. The billion-dollar Savings and Loans scandals that have occurred in America, whereby the executive directors of those institutions were able to rob their own banks, are but a few examples, the tip of an *Iceberg*. The screen that has so effectively captured the attention of anyone who might otherwise see, is that of Liberal Democracy, which, when baring itself, is the unabashed display of the "King who has no clothes." One impatiently awaits the innocence of youth to say: "Look! Look!" Unfortunately, an entire youth culture, preoccupied by portable video games that use as their marketing slogan: "Wherever you are, be somewhere else," assures a future of *individuals*, of historically unequalled passivity and complacent receptiveness. This, notwithstanding sporadic, vituperative and violent outbursts, which happen among those for whom assimilation has been unsuccessful.

Consequently, we ask: who will ask why, with Britain a leader in the European Community, NATO, and the United Nations, are Scottish and Irish people not allowed to have free lands? Why, with both Spain and France being leaders of great democracies, are the neighboring people of the Basque Nation not allowed to exist as such? Why are Palestinians refused all rights, classified as non-citizens and thereby *legally* excluded from their occupiers' constitution while being savagely subjected to genocide? Why is the country that is, unequivocally, the most violent nation on earth, with the most crime-infested cities, highest rates of murder and homicide and the ignored cries of poverty and racial-discrimination, allowed to swagger its bravado as the unchallenged Savior of World Peace? How is it that this Nation has been able to unleash its children, raised on television and video games, with no understanding of other people's cultures, languages and religions, to run amok in billion-dollar war toys that enable them to view the annihilation of human beings as home-runs, touchdowns and scores?

To answer those questions, we are given

predisposed opinions of the politically-*in*correct
organs, ETA, PLO, IRA, ETC. Being, as they are,
terrorist organizations whose indiscriminate abhorrent
acts of violence assure their causes to be securely
locked within a dialectic that can have only one correct
and acceptable position, a rigidly imposed stasis is
maintained. It is significant to note that in America, the
country employing, according to Jacques Ellul in
Propaganda, the most "highly effective programming of
public opinion" that no such lymph-node of dissent is
needed. Nevertheless, further protective measures
needed to ensure the invulnerability of the United
Stasis are accomplished by such men as Noam
Chomsky who rip the whole establishment of
government to shreds, tearing it limb from limb only to
reassure us in the end that democracy (the best of all
available systems) can and will still work. Not
surprisingly, Mr. Chomsky, the leftist-leaning liberal, is
extremely popular on university campuses throughout
the world. Nor is it surprising that he and other think-
tank analysts earn their pay as much from the inside of
government as out. These descendants of the Frankfurt
school provide a necessary outlet for the radicalism
and rebellion that the potentially disruptive element of
youth remains. The March 11th 1993 edition of *London
Student*, a newspaper widely circulated at University
College of London, prints a major article on Noam

Chomsky: "arguably the most important intellectual alive" and touted as (reprinted from *The Guardian*) "America's public enemy No. 1." Such accolades for the pre-eminent M.I.T. Professor of Linguistics, assure him his crown amongst the "radical" propensity of the student population.
BROADCAST ENDS

Pound wants to bring us around. He holds one end of the tally-stick and needs to pass it on. *Cohesion* is grasped for and there are too many fragments.

> I have brought the great ball of crystal;
> who can lift it?
> Can you enter the great acorn of light?
> ....
> Tho' my errors and wrecks lie about me.
> ....
> I cannot make it cohere.
> If love be not in the house there is nothing.
> The voice of famine unheard.

Canto CXVI

By this time, Pound had spoken to everybody from his closest circle of friends to world leaders. He had been caged in Pisa and confined at St. Elizabeth's.

This I had from Kalupso
          who had it from Hermes   ·

                              Canto CII

Here Hermes tells Calypso that Zeus himself has
said that she should let Odysseus pass. Pound and
Odysseus have from the beginning travelled as one and
now safe passage is sought.

                    and as to why Penelope waited
     keinas . . . e Orgei.
                              Canto CII

Penelope answers in the line Pound sends us to
complete ourselves: "Never at anytime did that man
harm anyone."
     Canto CII continues with an ideogram:
     [not or a *negative*] and then lines concerning his
friends:

不   But the lot of 'em, Yeats, Possum, Old Wyndham

          had no ground to stand on

was Pound's remark for what had been his insistence in

the 20s and 30s that they (W. B. Yeats, T. S. Eliot, and Lewis) failed to see that ignorance of money and how it should be issued prevented the creation of a society in which prosperity, culture and art could flourish.

The strength of men is in grain. 管 Kuan

NINE decrees, 8th essay, the Kuan 子 Tzu

Canto CVI

The first of the lines ends with the ideogram Kuan = "to govern" followed by the second ideogram Tzu = "the master" which when joined give us the acronym for the neo-Confucian Kuan Chung, minister of one of the provinces. The nine decrees and eighth essay refer to one of a series of thirty-two essays written by Kuan Chung that appeared after his death and all pertained to governance and the necessity to preserve agriculture and maintain the granaries—rhyming with an earlier line:

Barley is the marrow of men,

Canto CII

Both Canto CII and CVI play off two sympathetic *leitmotifs*. The first of the two refrains is that of the Elysian grain-rites: Demeter, mother of Persephone, who wore

the black dress of mourning because her lovely daughter
of spring and summer stayed captive in the Underworld
beneath the earth. Pound recognized the atayistic
remnants (black shawls) still worn in Venice (1908) when
he arrived there as a young poet of twenty-three,

I SAT on the Dogana's steps
   For the gondolas cost too much, that year

                                        Canto III

and lived on poorman's barley soup.

The second refrain, beginning with NINE *decrees*, is
from the descendent of Kung, elicited from the essays: (i)
"When the granaries have been filled, the people will
obey the laws and rules of *courtesy*." (ii) "Unless ordered
by God of the Sombre Heavens...none shall conduct a
military campaign, even for only one day." (iii) "Take care
of the aged who have lost their relatives, feed those who
are permanently ill, give shelter to helpless persons."

None of this should be mistaken for the "... Spew
Deal wangle ..." (Canto XCVII) of FDR's New Deal,
which Pound saw as playing politics with half-hearted
reforms, and what would be in today's pseudo-language
called "the 'tax-and-spend policies' of the Democrats,"
a.k.a. "band-aid tactics" of the Republicans.

The root of the disease is Usura and

with great difficulty got back to Paterson's
The bank makes it *ex nihil*

                              Canto XLVI

renting credit to nations with pederastic smirks all over
their faces. Pound wanted to know how many literate
senators there were, meaning who actually understood
money and its proper use. He wrote to Senator Cutting in
the States and received a reply that appears in the *Cantos*:

> "Eleven literates" wrote Senator Cutting,
>   "and, I suppose Dwight L. Morrow"
> Black shawls for Demeter.
> The cat talks—μάω— with a greek inflection,
>   Mohammed in sympathy: "is part of religion"

                              Canto XCVIII

Continuing from *Black shawls*, we recognize the
then-modern Italian custom passed on from Demeter. The
cat talks, I believe, through Dionysus as the Greek word
means "with desire or passion." Then Muhammed [*sic*],
peace and blessings upon him, is said to be in sympathy
with this as he says *desire* is part of religion.

The Prophet's passion would be "seek[ing] know-
ledge even unto China," (a famous quotation recorded in
the Hadeeth literature) together with his establishment of

strong local governments with an uncompromising pro-
hibition against usury. This prohibition is found in the
Koran and the Prophet himself likened usury to
committing fornication with one's mother in the shade of
the holy Kaba, an ancient ruin rebuilt by Abraham.

Looking back at these later Cantos: Rock Drill
(LXXXV-XCV) and Thrones (XCVI-CIX), we are in the
position of holding a great kaleidoscope seeking
perceptions and insights that might register the much-
sought-after "coherence" of the poet. The broken bits and
fragments that so characterized these cantos are best
described as Pound's attempt to construct a throne on
which God can sit.

> Belascio or Topaze, and not have it sqush,
> a "throne", something God can sit on
> without having it sqush;
>
> Canto LXXXVIII

A consensus is held by most Pound critics—Makin,
Davis, Kenner—that bits abound in great abundance for
what Pound himself called "a mosaic." Wyndham Lewis
described the Rock-Drill Cantos as "the relentless
hammering of Pound's mind," while Thrones intended
the moral and aesthetic "splendour of Just Rulers" (Peter
Makin's *Pound Cantos*), indicating that the *solid seat*

Topaz, God can sit on.

                          Canto CIV

is made manifest by light refracted from earthly gems.
Refuting their being fragmentary firmaments, Pound,
who had been engaged in a correspondence with the
Sinologist, Lewis Maverick, wrote

> Fragmentary:
>   (Maverick repeating this queery dogmaticly.
>   mosaic? any mosaic.
> You cannot leave these things out
>   Canto CV

Consequently, when we find lines like,

> Yao and Shun ruled by jade
>   Canto CVI

one must know where to look in order to see their exact
meaning. These chips of Chinese, possessing an intrinsic
beauty of their own in verse, nevertheless reflect an
historical reference to when jade was used as currency,
casting backwards the solid light of the Paradiso
"Thrones."
       It is noteworthy hearing what exists of subtle

harmony between what Pound, a master of literary criticism and precision, wrote about in his literary essay, "The Serious Artist."

"As there are in medicine the art of diagnosis and the art of cure, so in the arts, so in the particular arts of poetry and of literature, there is the art of diagnosis and there is the art of cure. They call one the cult of ugliness and the other the cult of beauty."

Pound continues:

"The cult of beauty is the hygiene, it is sun, air and the sea and the rain and the lake bathing. The cult of ugliness, Villon, Baudelaire, Corbière, Beardesley are diagnosis. Flaubert is diagnosis. Satire, if we are to ride this metaphore to staggers, satire is surgery, insertions and amputations.

"Beauty in art reminds one what is worth while. [...] You don't argue about an April wind, you feel bucked up when you meet it. You feel bucked up when you come on a swift moving thought in Plato [or Confucius] or on a fine line in a statue."

When Pound writes of usurious money-lenders, arms-merchants and monopolists, he employs a particular language. When he unsheathes the surgeon's scalpel to attack the evil root, *neschek*, he excels in the diagnostician's art, as the practitioner of the cult that splays open the foul and the foreboding.

All of what comes to us through Pound of the Chinese masters are ancient remedies good for all times, hence the cult of beauty expressed. This is equally true of the lucid and crisp constructs of beauty found in *The Cantos* or a piece of great art or a blustery autumn day. The poet's use of the dual craft of *melopœia* and *phanopœia*, upon which he too would hoist the sail of *logopœia* is the ship in which he moves. His discovery being that the Chinese ideograms may well be the most complete language form capable of expressing his experience.

IV

The Dantescan Motif

Dante's *Divina Commedia* was a gathering-in of past and present, representing what Pound would later define in terms of *cultural heritage*. Dante spoke of and for his time, embracing in his vision all of what he perceived of meanings, myths and Belief. The fact that he becomes part of our cultural heritage—though markedly diminished in an age in which all public discourse has been set in the "frame of entertainment" (Postman: *Amusing Ourselves to Death*), may find its best explanation in the Dantescan symbol for the universe, which was "the truth is not lost with velocity." Pound took it and said, "So age-old intelligence is not lost in an age of speed." What "we are" is "bedevilled by false diagnoses."

Dante's epic, written during the later years of the thirteenth century C.D., acknowledged the greatness of the earlier ages' poets. In reference to the preceding twelfth century, he honors the Provençal troubadour,

Arnaut Daniel, when in the twentieth canto of "The Purgatorio," Dante, on the tongue of the poet Guinizelli, says, "This one whom I point out with my finger [Daniel] was the better craftsman ("il miglior fabbro") in the mother tongue." Of all the troubadours, Daniel was Pound's favourite and when T. S. Eliot dedicated "The Wasteland," it was to Ezra Pound as *il miglior fabbro*.

In defining an epic, Pound said it was "a poem containing history." This leads us from Homer to Ovid (who retold the *stories* and *myths*) on to Dante who in writing his epic, elicited meanings of cultural (collective) importance, giving it, therefore, mythic proportions." The myth," as we would understand it from Walter Burkert:

> "The specific character of the myth seems to lie neither in the structure nor in the content of the tale, but in the use to which it is put: and this would be my final thesis:
>
> "Myth is a traditional tale with secondary, partial references to something of collective importance."

(Burkert as quoted by I. Dallas, *Oedipus and Dionysus.*)

Pound gathered in, as did Dante, collected, as Confucius collected the *Odes*, and told a poem....

The centrifugal force of Dante's writing emanates out across the orb of Pound's odyssey, bringing us in contact with our (true) heritage. Similarly, in all that

Dante told of, we are to listen to what he taught. Stressed in the meter of his colloquial Italian tongue, he says, "*Ex diffinentium cognitone diffinate resultat cognito.*" (Knowledge of a definite thing comes from knowledge of things defined.) Confucius to Dante. Likewise, adding force to Pound's war against the crime of the centuries, *usura*, we hear Dante damn the usurers to the same circle of Hell as the sodomites, because both act against the potential abundance of Nature. Dante echoes most clearly the condemnation of the Church, according to its now discarded Canon Law, of those who practise usury and sodomy as a pair to one hell for the same reason: both acts are against natural increase. In Pound's Canto XLV, we can hear again, both in meaning and meter, those reverberations.

> Usura slayeth the child in the womb
> It stayeth the young man's courting
> It hath brought palsey to bed, lyeth
> between the young bride and her bridegroom.
>   CONTRA NATURAM

Dante utilized an earlier work of art, a sculptured panel by Cosima Tura, which consisted of three separate compartments, to construct his poetic vision trilogy. The upper compartment of Tura's piece depicts the "Triumph of Love" and the "Triumph of Chastity." The second, middle frame shows the zodiacal signs, while the lower one depicts known local events from Tura's day. Tura's composition noticeably corresponds to Dante's Paradiso, Purgatorio and Inferno. Pound utilizes the Dantescan model as a *motif* in his *Cantos*, while not following it as his structure. When we hear certain themes within Pound's work that relate to those of Dante, sometimes using the chosen Italian while at others only the metric scale and style of the previous poet transposed into English, we experience recall. For example there are the Hell and Throne Cantos and similar themes, displaying a panoply of correlative interplay which weaves Dante into Pound's poem. Thereby, we have the Paradiso Cantos, replete with their heroes: men of good government and champions of social and cultural elevation. Next, there are the cantos of transfiguration in which the dynamics of change occur, illustrated by Pound's drawing upon Ovid's *Metamorphosis*. This is where Pound refers to the tale of the tribe, [the tribe of Adam], which is "an account of man's progress from darkness to light." He refers to this as *semina motuum* ("seed in motion"), from Dante. In this middle zone of transformation and transmutation, we can recognize those cantos where the gods are acting through man's mind and perceptions making manifest his intelligence, his love (*amo ergo sum*—Pound's *Dantesque* letterhead on his stationery at St. Elizabeth's), perception of beauty, sense of mystery, his power and urge to make (music, painting, poetry and prose) and, lastly, that aspiration directed toward a *paradiso terrestre.*

Reflecting on Pound's earthly paradise, I am reminded of the phrase used to describe the city of Madinah during the lifetime of the prophet Muhammad and the years immediately after his death, which was, "Al-Madinah al-Munawwarah." This reference to an *illuminated city,* sixth century C.D., is in its being inhabited by enlightened people, for whom worship of The Real (observance of rituals passed from the ancients) was their pivotal axis and the uncompromising ban on any form of usury their safeguard against its cell-attacking disease.

The third zone of cantos, corresponding directly to Dante's Inferno and at the same time like Tura's panel depicting events of his day, are the Hell Cantos. Pound did not limit his *hell* to events only of his day, although the most famous of "hell cantos" are XIV and XV of which he wrote to Wyndham Lewis, "Hell Cantos: You will readily see that the 'hell' is a portrait of contemporary England, or at least Eng. as she wuz when I left her." [London, 1919-1920]

> Above the hell-rot
> the great arse-hole,
> broken with piles,
> hanging stalactites,
> greasy as sky over Westminster,
>
> Canto XIV

the soil living pus, full of vermin,
dead maggots begetting live maggots,
  slum owners,
usurers squeezing crab-lice, panders to authority,
pets-de-loup, sitting on piles of stone books,
obscuring the texts with philology,
  hiding them under their persons,
         Canto XIV

Further on in the *Cantos*, Pound informs us of hellish events taking place in America during the Wilson and Roosevelt presidencies. As *leitmotifs* they appear as early as Canto II in the mentioning of "the darkness of hell" and in describing a scene where a fair young boy named Lyaeus (Dionysus) is sold into slavery by money-hungry and short-sighted merchant sailors.

I have seen what I have seen.
  When they brought the boy I said:
"He has a god in him,
  though I do not know which god."
And they kicked me into the fore-stays.
         Canto II

The three-ply model used by Dante in the Divine Comedy charts the course of a man's ascent from Inferno to Paradise in the form of a long narrative that Pound draws into his *Cantos* as *motif* while holding to a similar periplus for his traveller. In both poems, the respective poets are synonymous with that traveller. Odysseus/ Pound found himself in the muck of despicable conditions in a usurious world and searched for the way to get the hell out.

"Hoggers of harvest are the curse of the people." A non-visible financial oligarchy controls the visible world, making life (and the journey) difficult.

Sodom on Thames sold out Napoleon.'
Canto CV

Jacob Rothschild, based in Paris, was able to get word to his brother Nathan, in London, before anyone else knew, of the results of the Battle of Waterloo. The English banker went immediately to the newspaper and told them the British had lost. As the news broke, the Rothschilds in England began to sell heavy which set off a panic on the London market from fear that the French would soon be moving in. Before closing time on the exchange market, Nathan Rothschild bought back everything he could get his hands on, earning an unprecedented 150 million dollars in 1815. Alas, the war against usury un-won summons Dante's invocation:

And from far
> il tremolar della marina
>> [Purgatorio 1-116-7]
>> ["the trembling of the sea"]

into Pound's Canto XCII to purify himself from ungodly acts.

Having made the *climb* from hell through purgatory on up to Paradiso, we see the souls of just and temperate rulers as so many lights that gradually arrange themselves in order to form the first sentence from Dante's Book of Wisdom: DILIGITE IUSTITIAM QUI IUDICATIS TERRAM–("Love righteousness, you that are judges on earth.") Hence, all of the heroes of Pound's *Cantos* are men of good government, rulers who gave precise verbal definitions and "put a bridle on usury." They were those who demanded solid money, "ruled by jade," and in prohibiting (even if sometimes only by condemnation–Jefferson, Adams, Van Buren) usurious practices, were elevated to the stature of homeric heroes. Picking up from the last letter in the word TERRAM ("earth") from the line quoted above, it is discovered that in Dante's manuscript it gradually transformed into the shape of an eagle: the symbol for JUSTICE. In an age of fascinating computer graphics this may be over-shadowed, while as a poetic image its meaning can hardly be surpassed.

As it is my view that Pound's theorem on the agreement that will exist between men of knowledge, · regardless of the varying times and places in which they lived, is true, it is imperative to seek new Terrain. The highest rôle for man is to point towards those of knowledge. **"There came a man running from the furthest part of the city calling: 'follow the Messengers,'"** is a verse from the Koran that points to a person who will speak up. When Dante speaks through his Divine Comedy, engaging us in sublime metaphor and myth it requires one to reject the scrappy remains of dubiously edited and *revised* Judaeo-Christian journalism. From Pound's essay, "The Ethics of Mencius," he states: "Jehovah is a semitic cuckoo's egg laid in the European nest. He has no connection with Dante's god–That latter concept of supreme Love and Intelligence is certainly not derived from the Old Testament." In the same essay, Pound says: "It is mere shouting for the hometeam that so-called Christian virtues were invented A.D. 1 to A.D. 32 in Judea," and follows-up with an example.

"If a man died in a ditch Shun felt it as if he had killed him." (This of the Emperor Shun)

"Is there," said Mang Tsze (Mencius), "any difference between killing a man with a club and a sword?"

"No," said King Hwuy.
"Is there any difference between killing him with
a sword and with a system of government?"

However easy it might be to recognize what could
be seen as Christian virtues in the fourth century B.C.
parable of Mencius, what survives of biblical folklore
does not contain nearly enough grist or clear direction.
What does remain, despite the disincorporation of Christ,
is the one brilliant anecdote, surviving the overly-zealous
editors' circumcisional scissors, where Jesus, *peace be
upon him*, violently expurgated the *squalid* money
changers from the sacred temple. Dante certainly held
nothing back when condemning the usurers and those
that commit fraud. As we know by now, Ezra let them
have it.

V

The Volitionists

IN 1901 at the age of sixteen, Pound set off for the University of Pennsylvania where, in his own words, as "a lanky whey-faced youth" he began what could be mustered of a classical education. He read Catullus, Browning and Dowson, and in 1902, met a fellow student by the name of William Carlos Williams. Williams, who wrote among many books, *In the American Grain*, one of the most superb pieces of poetic prose in the English language, remained a faithful friend throughout his life.

In 1903, both young men left Pennsylvania to study at Hamilton College at Clinton in New York. We know from Williams that Pound was soon known as "a character," characterized by his restless, self-conscious and nervous nature. After a two-year course in Anglo-Saxon and Romance languages along with medieval history Pound returned to the University of Pennsylvania to complete his postgraduate studies. It was during this period that he met Hilda Doolittle, better known as the poet H. D., who was Pound's first true affection. She said of him: "He was immensely sophisticated, immensely superior, immensely rough and ready...One would dance with him for what he might say!"

Pound completed his studies, made a short trip to Europe (he had been twice before as an adolescent with an aunt); and upon his return took up a post at Wabash College in Crawfordville, Indiana. Not surprisingly, he did not fit in at the rather staid mid-western American college and a year later in 1908 was expelled after it was discovered that he had kind-heartedly helped out a young actress-in-distress by allowing her to take meals with him and once spend the night on an extra cot in his rooms. He left for Venice and

> I sat on the Dogana's steps
> For the gondolas cost too much, that year,

and passed what he recalled as one of the happiest times of his life. During those months while living on next to nothing, Pound published his first volume of poems, called *A Lume Spento*, for eight dollars that were left from the eighty dollars he had arrived in Italy with. Before the year was out, he headed for London to meet W. B. Yeats, the man he had decided was the only great living poet.

Quickly becoming known in London literary circles

as the extroverted American with nineteenth-century romantic tastes in literature, he finally met his hero, Yeats. He soon, in fact, met everybody who was worth knowing. His meeting with Wyndham Lewis, his strongest and most extraordinary life-long friend, was depicted as two tough bull-dogs squaring off to one another. He met the other expatriated American, T. S. Eliot, who also endured trials of brotherhood and intimate collaboration that spanned more than fifty years. After Pound's first meeting with Lawrence, the English writer exclaimed that E. P. was "a genius." Upon their second meeting, Lawrence's view digressed as he claimed Pound was somewhat "of a mountebank" and altogether too cocky.

In 1909, Pound met Ford Maddox Ford, a literary mentor and publisher of London's emergent young writers. He took Pound in and helped him get his poems in print while at the same time working to free up his style in order to enter the twentieth century. The ten years that followed may well be the most exciting and radical decade of this century's literature. It gave birth to James Joyce, whose first novel Pound helped to get serialized in a literary magazine. It gave us the young Eliot's best works as well as the laughing lion, Wyndham Lewis, whose Vorticist Movement brought the best writers and artists in Europe together to BLAST the establishment. When Pound met the economic theorist, Major C. H. Douglas, in 1918, a great many of Pound's disgusts with the commercial system of art and the defilement of social and business practices were not only confirmed, but given what was to be the most important *core* element that would help shape all his future work.

This brief biographical sketch has been to introduce MR. C. H. DOUGLAS. The focus will now move to Douglas and his principles as they influenced and shaped Pound's. Likewise, the effects of Douglasism were not limited to one set of ideas, but provided additional impetus for Pound to seek a variety of models and methods pertaining to monetary systems, methods of trading and creating open, accessible markets.

The period of history in which Pound and Douglas first met and then continued to work in tandem was a time of massive global convolutions and upheavals. It started with the years immediately preceding the First World War and then the aftermath which was not less than the coming on of the Second. Pound insistently tells us that all wars are created for the benefit of the usurers: "Usurocracy makes wars in succession. It makes them according to a pre-established plan for the purpose of creating debts." (*The Enemy Is Ignorance.*) Pound goes on in the same essay to nail a notice to the wall:

A NATION
THAT WILL NOT
GET ITSELF INTO DEBT
DRIVES THE USURERS
TO FURY

It was during those years of war boom prosperity that the ideas of Douglas took hold in Pound's creative imagination. As the war-machine gears up, new jobs are created, weapons contractors make a killing and trade swings into high action. Governments borrow heavy, the *pump is primed*, fuelled with the blood of nineteen-year-olds. The banks are making it hand-over-fist. A quarter of a century later, in November 1945, while Pound stepped off a government plane in Washington D.C., with his legs shackled and his hands cuffed, emaciated after months of being caged in Pisa at the American Disciplinary Training Center, David Rockefeller stepped off a private jet in Moscow (before the signing of Treaties) to set up loans to the anti-capitalist Soviets, providing the necessary capital for the biggest military (Cold War) build-up in world history.

Returning to the 1920s, we can enter into the setting within which Douglas presented his economic theorem that refuted both the Marxist, as well as the capitalist, view.

Io venni in luogo d'ogni luce muto

Canto XIV

"I arrive into this place (where I am) of silenced light," is a line spoken from Hell—London—by Pound to herald the next stage.

D OUGLAS' theorem was purposefully expressed in terms used by Marx to demonstrate his antithetical conclusions. Douglas, as well as the economist Gesell (who developed the principle of "stamp-script") objected to Marx on the basis that he had "nothing to criticize in money." For Marx, the bank (primary organ of the capitalist system) was a given. Douglas named his model The A plus B Theorem, which stated that sufficient purchasing power must be in the hands of people. Unlike Marx, both Douglas and Pound were not opposed to Profit (P), which is the just reward for good producers, not for monopolists, bankers and manipulators of values. Douglas stated that the *price charged* for a given product must be equal to A: All payments made to individuals in the form of wages, salaries, and dividends, plus B: all payments made to other organizations such as material suppliers, banks and other [hidden] costs. He then goes on to tell us that fairness cannot exist under the present system as banks charge both individuals and nations alike for the use of purchasing power and take most of that money, created *ex nihil*, out of circulation or concentrate it amongst an élite few, thereby diminishing the ability of those who work (and receive A), from ever being able to afford what they need. Banks and credit companies take full advantage by providing additional credit (cards, etc.), encouraging deficit spending and ever widening the gap between prices (V) and A plus B. This is *usura*, a definition of which I provided earlier from Pound's footnote at the end of Canto XLV: "Usury: A charge for the use of purchasing power, levied without regard to production; often without regard to the possibilities of production."

This material shows up in Canto XXXVIII in a fairly direct reprint of Douglas' words. The first of two successive passages quotes Douglas' refutation that what he was proposing was a fixed amount of cash being sufficient for a nation's needs.

"I have of course never said that the cash is constant
(Douglas) and in fact, the population (Britain, 1914)
was left with 800 millions of 'deposits' after all cash had been drawn, and
these deposits were satisfied by the
            printing of treasury notes."

His point being not that additional money (tickets) could not be printed, but who should have the benefit of this. We know for sure that both he and Pound believed it should not be the private-interest group of the banking élite. It was the premise of C. H. Douglas that if a nation controlled its own money and credit, the enormous benefits would bring not only an end to taxes, but provide *dividends* to be given back to the community.

An' the fuzzy bloke sez (legs no pants wd. fit) 'IF
that is so, any government worth a damn can
pay dividends?'
The major chewed it a bit and sez: 'Y—es, eh...
You mean instead of collectin' taxes?'
'Instead of collecting taxes.'

Canto XLVI

Here there is an internal rhyming with meanings
expressed by the neo-Confucian rulers within the *Cantos*,
who provided a form of *share* back to the community
rather than allow state officials to stuff their own pockets
and create a bloated bureaucracy. As well as that we can
hear outside on the street: "Governance without State—
Commerce without Usury!" This slogan has come down
from the *anarch* and composer Richard Wagner during his
participation in the Revolution of 1849 while in Dresden.
This battle cry might well have remained buried had it
not been heard in Birmingham, England (October 1992),
while used by a movement, celebrating their Celtic
heritage, with representatives from the outer Hebrides to
the coast of Galicia. These folks inaugurated an "open
market" trading fair where freshly minted gold and silver
coins were introduced AS MONEY!, bearing the inscrip-
tion: "Emir-el-Moumenin." This same *inscription*, used by
Abd-el-Melik in 692 C.D. and carried far into Europe,

reads the same in Canto XCVII. The historical event of this *fair* cannot be underrated. When poetry moves into action, we know that it can purport powerful changes.

Returning to the thirty-eighth Canto, and taking up the second passage lifted from the Douglasonian A plus B Theorem text:

> A factory
> has also another aspect, which we call the financial aspect
> It gives people the power to buy (wages, dividends
> which are power to buy) but it is also the cause of prices
> or values, financial, I mean financial values
> It pays workers, and pays *for* material.
> What it pays in wages and dividends
> stays fluid, as power to buy, and this power is less,
> per forza, damn blast your intellex, is less
> than the total payments made by the factory
> (as wages, dividends AND payments for raw material
> bank charges, etcetera)
> and all, that is the whole, that is the total
> of these is added into the total of prices
> caused by that factory, any damn factory
> and there is and must be therefore a clog
> and the power to purchase can never
> (under the present system) catch up with
> prices at large,

and the light became so bright and so blindin'
in this layer of paradise
   that the mind of man was bewildered.
                         Canto XXXVIII

The Douglas *era*, unknown to all but a few careful readers, is more *commonly* called "the time of John Maynard Keynes–world famous economist." Pound arranges in Canto XXII for a conversation between the two. The initials C. H. are obviously Douglas's and Keynes is referred to as both Mr. Bukos and Mr. H. B., while the euphemism H.C.L. is High Cost of Living. The excerpted lines that follow now speak clearly for themselves.

And C. H. said to the renowned Mr. Bukos:
"What is the cause of the H.C.L.? and Mr. Bukos,
The economist consulted of nations, said:
                  "Lack of labour."
And there were two millions of men out of work.
And C. H. shut up, he said
He would save his breath to cool his own porridge,
But I didn't, and I went on plaguing Mr. Bukos
Who said finally: "I am an orthodox
"Economist."
        Jesu Christo!

The next two lines read:

Standu nel paradiso terrestre
Pensando come si fesse compagna d'Adamo!!

They translate, following the expletive: "Standing in the Earthly paradise / Thinking as he made a companion of Adam."
The dialogue closes with a Poundian quote from Keynes.

And Mr. H. B. wrote in to the office:
I would like to accept C. H.'s book
But it would make my own seem so out of date.

Canto XXII

This concludes the references to Douglas. Yet the implications from the budget initiatives of his antithetical nemesis, Keynes, spill over into Pound's complaint that among the many possible good jobs wasted are those of artists and writers who can't get into print. The huge publishing house, the Macmillan Company, founded its fortune on masses of stodgy Victorian poetics that clogged the way for people like Pound, Joyce, Eliot, Lewis and Lawrence. Francis Turner Palgrave, a critic and professor at Oxford (1885-1895), compiled such an anthology, called *The Golden Treasury of the Best Songs and Lyrical Poems in the English Language.*

[...]   The whole fortune of
Mac Narpen and Company is founded
Upon Palgrave's Golden Treasury. Nel paradiso terrestre

And all the material was used up, Jesu Christo,
And everything in its place, and nothing left over
To make una compagna d'Adamo. Commi si fesse?

Canto XXII

["To make a mate for Adam. How to make her?"]

From seeking available models, within which Pound saw possibilities of a way out and the ascent from the dark labyrinth, he did not desist. From the "jade" of Shun to the Tuscan coins made available by Ferdinando, who established the Monte dei Paschi as a lending institution to provide credit without usury, to the silver *dirhems* of the Caliph Abdal-Malik introduced up to the gates of Vienna and on to the modern times of Douglas and Gesell, Pound continually affirmed that there were ways to break the spell. That spell leaves most people sinking sickened into the pits of their stomachs, feeling powerless to change what appears to be the most pervasive and powerful of systems.

Silvio Gesell's "Stamp-Script" was one such later model and though its use was cut short in the small town of Wörgl in the Austrian Tyrol, it did function to raise a whole community up from ruin in the early 1930s. "The town had been bankrupt: the citizens had not been able to pay their rates, the municipality had not been able to pay their schoolteachers, etc. But in less than two years, everything had been put right and the townspeople had even built a new stone bridge [and improved a local hospital]. All went well until an ill-starred Wörgl note was presented at the counter of an Innsbruck bank. It was noticed, all right—no doubt about that. The plutocratic monopoly had been infringed. Threats, fulmination, anathema! The burgomaster was deprived of his office, but the ideological war had been won." (*Visiting Card*, E. Pound, 1942.)

What had taken place was that the mayor of Wörgl, faced with crippling economic conditions (caused by major banks shrinking the amount of cash in circulation), implemented, by his own initiative, the printing of money to which a one percent face value stamp needed to be affixed each month. The idea being that the money would stay moving, as hoarding it up and sitting on it would result in a loss of one percent each month. There-. fore, money was kept in circulation, with *no-one paying any taxes* except the one percent, and only if you had the currency in your pocket. Within two years a mini-boom had taken place, bringing tremendous benefit to all the townsfolk until, alas, a Wörgl note showed up in an Innsbruck bank.

> the state need not borrow
> as was shown by the mayor of Wörgl
> who had a milk route
> and whose wife sold shirts and short breechers
> and on whose book-shelf was the Life of Henry Ford
> and also a copy of the Divina Commedia
> and of the Gedichte of Heine
> a nice little town in the Tyrol in a wide flat-lying valley
> near Innsbruck and when a note of the
> small town of Wörgl went over
> a counter in Innsbruck
> and the banker saw it go over
> all the slobs in Europe were terrified
>
> Canto LXXIV

The Tyrolian town was, according to Pound, the only valid use of the Gesellist system, while a ludicrous misuse took place in Canada later on. Gesell, himself, was once appointed Minister of Finance in the Bavarian government just after the first World War. Unfortunately, the government was almost immediately infiltrated and taken over by communists, which, by his implication in that government, after the reds were violently purged, led to Gesell being tried for *treason*. He defended himself in an eloquent speech that laid out the monetary and *land reforms* which he had tried to implement. Gesell's speech ended with the lines: "The right of the whole collective proceeds of labor implies the abolition of all unearned income, i.e. interest and rent of credit," emphasizing that all could go well if money and land were removed from the domain of special privilege and as opportunities for USURY. The Germans not only acquitted him, but found considerable merit in his work.

The cross reference between Gesell and his being mixed up with the communists and Pound who whole-heartedly supported Mussollini's attempts to curtail the power of the banks as well as introduce innovative land reforms, "draining the marshes—public works for the benefit of people," strikes a harmonic chord. Pound's support for those "so provident laws" of the modern Italian leader, rhymes with Canto XLIV—which honors Ferdinando III, 1749-1841, who worked to bridle usury. Correspondence and dialogue with influential Italian ministers, such as Odon Por (as well as American congressmen), who would listen to his ideas, earned Pound the title of traitor in his own country.

There is one last anecdote to cap off the volitionist tactics of Ezra Pound, all of which (in view) arose out of what proceeded "whenever the Rothschild and other gents in the gold business have gold to sell, and raise the price." Pound elaborates further: "The public is fooled by propaganda about devaluation of the dollar or other monetary units according to the country chosen to be victimized. The argument is that the high price of the monetary unit is injurious to the nation's commerce.

"But when the nation, that is the people of the nation, own the gold and the financiers own the dollars or other monetary units, the gold standard is restored. This *raises the value* of the dollar and the citizens of 'rich' nations, as well as citizens of other nations, are diddled." (*An Introduction to the Economic Nature of the United States.*)

We have now the anecdote of Thaddeus Coleman Pound, Ezra's grandfather, an entrepreneur and businessman who actively engaged in the political life of his time, pursuing government initiatives that were both good for people, as well as the land. Pound discovered, while in Rapallo, that among other things, his grandfather was an ardent proponent of *monetary reform* who engaged in vibrant correspondence with prominent senators and congressmen [just as his grandson would do two generations later] whom he believed could legislate such reforms.

Mr. Pound Sr.'s most prestigious feat was to build a railway line across Wisconsin, which he did with $5000 cash and credit from a timber merchant who would receive all the trees cut to clear a path for the railway. Thaddeus printed his own money that he used to pay his lumberjacks and rail-layers and which was good for all dry goods, food stuffs, hardware and timber from the general store set up for the men and their families, and which was backed by the value of the timber cut, like I just said, to open a passage for the tracks. There was an aristocracy among these frontiersmen and it was a physical aristocracy. Pound wrote: "My grandfather used to wrestle with his lumberjacks not only for sport, but to maintain his prestige." (*An Introduction to the Economic Nature of the United States.*)

Thaddeus accomplished his goal, but like many independent, hardworkin' men, he soon found himself under-the-gun of special privilege and was railroaded out of the lumber (American for timber) business. He was pushed out by Frederick Weyerhaeuser, the American capitalist dubbed the "Lumber-King" who purchased one million acres of timberland in Washington and Oregon from the Northern Pacific Railroad. Canto XXII begins with: "An' that man..." which is Pound's grandfather.

A N' that man sweat blood
to put through that railway,
And what he ever got out of it?
And he said one thing: As it costs,
As in any indian war it costs the government

20,000 dollars per head
To kill off the red warriors, it might be more humane
And even cheaper, to educate.
And there was the other type, Warenhauser,
That beat him, and broke up his business,
Tale of the American Curia that gave him,
Warenhauser permission to build the Northwestern railway
And to take the timber he cut in the process;
So he cut a road through the forest,
Two miles wide, an' perfectly legal.
Who wuz agoin' to stop him!

                                                      Canto XXII

The double-deal hockers of the Gold Standard in America are invariably opposed to Douglas's, Gesell's and Thaddeus Pound's initiatives to print. Two essential points need to be clear. A "gold-standard" does not suppress paper, but "theoretically" backs it while both paper and gold are allowed to fluctuate in the hands of the bankers. Private speculators whose control over the Nation's resources are never, at no time, abrogated, benefit from "all human exchange of goods be[ing] bottlenecked through gold [*i.e.* the Gold Standard]." (Rome Radio Broadcast, January, 1942.)

More deserving of response would be the contemporary economist, Umar Vadillo, who, in his *Fatwa on*

Paper Money (Madinah Press, 1991) stands firm that the bank note itself is worthless and unacceptable:

Origin of Paper Money
As a Promissory Note Based on a Deposit

"Originally, paper money was a receipt which represented a certain amount of real-money, usually gold or silver, given to the goldsmith. Paper money then was not legal currency (imposed by the law of the state) but it uniquely represented a contract whereby a deposit of money (like a debt) was recognized with the goldsmith. Usually the reason for this kind of contract was the desire to keep the gold (or silver) in a safe place with the goldsmith. When the gold was deposited with the goldsmith, they would issue in return a receipt whereby the goldsmith admitted that he held the money of the depositor. Very soon, something started to happen with the receipts. If a client wanted to buy something and he had some receipts, why should he go to the goldsmith to exchange them if he could buy directly with them? The last was much easier. The merchant, at the same time, decided to pay his suppliers with the same receipts. Thus, paper was in circulation, albeit, limitedly. At a certain point, the goldsmith said to himself: 'Although many people can exchange the receipts for the gold, not all of them do it at the same time, so I could just lend receipts for a period of time and nobody would notice. Because the receipts are like the gold, I can create money out of nothing and lend it at interest.' Thus, the principle of banking started. The banks started to appear everywhere. Some of them grew. Some of them that were too greedy collapsed.

"Another evolutionary step occurred when the concept of a national bank was created. It was going to be the bank of banks. The first one was the Bank of England (1694). Its founder, William Paterson, explained it in this way: 'The bank will benefit from the interest of the money that it creates out of nothing.' The relation between the bank and the establishment of paper-money as the medium of exchange is essential. One could not have happened without the other."

Elaborating on Vadillo's simple explanation from sources found in both his and Pound's essays, we can add that through the passage of laws, congressional and parliamentary, banks have added to their hand a few more cards.

The bank receives as deposits from numerous *John Thrifties* "monies" which it first records as assets. Then, needing to only have a very small percent on hand for withdrawals, it records them again as resources available to be lent out at interest. Therefore, they double it and, what's more, are allowed *by law* to multiply it by eight or ten over actual deposited amounts with BENEFIT, as stated by Paterson. If that ain't the damnedest! Now, on top of that, can you figure that when the banks lend to your government, the debit gets posted as an asset in the banks' books which, AGAIN, they, BY LAW, can rent out? All this passed into law by "the slough of unamiable liars," (Canto XIV), voted into high office "By the People." Now that's a bitch, and when the *goberment* cannot pay, they raise yr taxes, for the guarantor isn't the bank after all but "the back" of the community. That works out, according to my figures, to a lot of sore folks.

I see clearly Vadillo's authoritative statements, while acknowledging all of Pound's forays deep into the shed of the twentieth century. Each of Pound's rescue remedies were in the face of very real obstacles. He pulled examples from Chinese jade to the Umayyad Caliph Abdalmalik, whose adjustment, in 692 C.D., to a weight ratio of 6.5 to 1 of silver to gold, (based on the Prophet's decree in the sixth century) was introduced into Europe in the face of Roman decline and gross economic disparity. This adjustment directly improved the lot of ordinary people who had silver, while an overspent ruling class primarily held gold.

Melik & Edward struck coins-with-a-sword,
"Emir el Moumenin" (Systems p.134)
    six and $^1/_2$ to one, or the sword of the Prophet,
Silver being in the hands of the people

                              Canto XCVII

Alexander Del Mar, Pound's primary source on *The History of Money*, affirmed that it was the abuse of money that weakened Roman rule, which would lead one to believe that the Muslims reversed the cycle of history by putting it right. Del Mar seemed to think it was some sort of very clever bribe or trick on the part of the Believers to get people to join up. Something like: Worship God alone, establish trust and "brotherly deference," abolish taxes (except what is specifically for the poor: *Zakat*) and, in general, be afforded a better life by the silver in your pocket. Damn clever trick, coulda fooled me.

The fact remains that Pound did not stop with tokens of intrinsic worth, but when confronted by barriers, moved on to printed material. The radical thesis of Umar Vadillo, vis-a-vis the 1990s, needs an arena in which it can work, just as Thaddeus Pound's venture needed the ol' General Store where the "bearer shall receive goods to the value of." That needed arena being an open market allowing free trade where producers and manufacturers themselves, or their agents or partners (who need not own anything but a good name) can bring stuffs to the market at wholesale prices directly to folks AND who will all trade, exchange, buy n' sell with real money.

If I am walking around London with a gold coin in my pocket and if I cannot use it to purchase a railway ticket, then one may have to be patient with that in revolutionary times. If, on the other hand, I cannot get a loaf of bread and a cup of barley soup, well, I'm stuck. The fact that my brother and I went into a Portuguese *patisserie* off London's Portobello Road and I said to the proprietor:

"This is a silver coin. Will you accept it as money?"

And she sez, holding it in her hand, "What do you want for it?"

I say "due cappuccini."

"And two cakes?"

"But of course!" Marie Antoinette, you're my kinda gal.

We can only conclude that the harm done to modern man, by the results of usura have been *tres mal*. The pound of flesh that Shakespeare's Shylock wanted weren't no "elbow or knee cap" but the poor fellow's means of natural increase. The proliferation of present-day eunuchs is certainly enough to make your hair stand on end. It is no wonder women these days are up in arms. Unfortunately, one abnormality leads to another which is possibly why many women today are strutting around like they've got padded pelvic bones to go with those big shoulders. People of the poorer countries in the world (whose boundaries now include increasingly large portions of depressed Europe) do not have the luxury of such *haute couture*. Insurmountable debts, devalued currencies, theft of their natural resources against the rising cost of imports along with the rampant proliferation of deadly crime, have women from traditional backgrounds as well as those courageous enough to stand clear of the consumer currents within modern society more concerned about the safety of their families and the protection of our *Earth*.

In the 30th of January 1993 edition of the London *Times*, we have a current example that affirms the validity of continuing Pound's efforts and rhymes with his belief that the Church, unfettered by modern innovations, had a rôle to play:

BISHOPS CONDEMN RUN
ON IRELAND'S CURRENCY

BY JANET BUSH
TIMES ECONOMICS CORRESPONDENT

A GROUP of Ireland's most influential Roman Catholic bishops yesterday condemned currency speculators, who last week launched a fearsome attack on the Irish punt, as having held the nation to ransom.

Bishop Michael Smith said: "This damages the country's future and is at the expense of the common good. It cannot be condoned and is contrary to any Christian principle."

A little more than a hundred and fifty years earlier, 1819, another Irish priest, Father Jeremiah O'Callaghan, from Ross Carberry, Cork, kicked up a storm by refusing a man his *last rites* and Sacraments until he remit to all his customers what he had gained from them through usury. The man who sold flax seed, worth nine shillings at sowing time on delayed payment for twelve shillings and sixpence at harvest time, complied with Father O'Callaghan's demand and, furthermore, had it written into his *will* that this should be announced publicly to the local congregation after his death. Father O'Callaghan's unwillingness to let things slide into the "bog" of *neschek*, *i.e.*, categorically contra the Church's Canon Law, resulted in his being sacked from his parish and ostracized by the Holy Church. The priest who twice, unsuccessfully, petitioned the Pope, having travelled all the way to Rome, finally founded a small parish in Vermont. Undoubtedly, O'Callaghan left a legacy, however much buried, amongst the Irish.

Bishop Smith's remarks, as quoted in the Times, are long overdue and while showing a bit of mettle have only a faint echo of his predecessor's ardent fervour. The prolonged silence from the Vatican in regards to the absolutely clear and irrefutable prohibition of usury, contrasting greatly with the noisy rumblings of corruption involved in their own banking practices, implicates the modern church of Rome as open accomplices in this most heinous of crimes.

THE WORDS of Rev. Smith bring to a close the theme of Volitionism and kicks off the note of COUNTERPOINT:

"Economic habits arise from the nature of things (animal, mineral, vegetable). Economic mess, evil theories are due to failure to keep the different nature of different things clearly distinct in the mind," (*ABC of Economics*), and a straight shot to Confucius. Hence, Malik ibn Anas gives all the rules and gradations, in specifics, for the acceptable methods of trading, buying and selling of perishable and non-perishable goods, those crafted by labor, those bred, those exchanged by means of a contractual relationship in which one partner does not own, but can sell, etc.

Producing a useful item—say a broom—can be a good business, if you realistically make a quantity people need to use and price them according to their real cost, including a fair profit. AND you pay out to workers a sufficient amount of money which is reflected in the price of the things they need and want to buy, AND remove the special privilege given banks to rent credit to manufacturers and thereby take back out of circulation the necessary money needed to facilitate buying and selling. According to the present system, people who are paid to do a job can't afford to buy the things they themselves make, and need from what others like them make. This is because of the ADDED COST of Rent, removed from circulation or centralized among an élite few who then can create a monopoly. The GAP widens continually and additional credit is provided as vasoline at interest rates sometimes approaching thirty percent.

The brief paraphrasing of Sections VI-IX of *The ABC of Economics* draws on Douglas and more as Pound insists that intelligence must accompany any realistic system. He had already told us in the opening chapter of *Economics* that: "No economic system is worth a hoot without 'goodwill'. No intelligent system of economics will function unless people are prepared to act on their understanding." What is to be avoided is letting criminals hold our money and do with it whatever they like. "The criminal classes have no intellectual interest." Those who say they have *"le droit de faire tout ce qui ne nuit pas aux autres,"* are precisely those who are not to be trusted.

In Part Five, Minor Addenda and Varia, of the *ABC's,* Pound says: "There is nothing to be said against a gang of thieves playing poker except that they are playing with other men's money." He refers here to STOCKBROKERS, handy partners in crime with bankers, whose bets and limits are not put up with any consultation from the communities whose funds they hold. Mr. Keating of the Lincoln Savings and Loan scandal, who pushed junk bonds off on Ma and Pa Kettle, seems to fit the shoe. What contribution these high rollers have made to their countries, patriots though they be, come up short as they "so far haven't been able to dig up even a journalistic liar to write them a tombstone." (*ABC of Economics*.) Probably this is why Mr. Robert Maxwell, financier, publisher and wheeler-dealer extraordinaire of other people's money had to be buried in Israel, on top of Mount Zion, its holiest site. Maxwell's contribution to Britain will long be remembered as the man of *humble beginnings* who came from the east as a poor immigrant, made millions, and left millions considerably poorer. The man who changed his religion to that of the Church of England, left us with those immortal words from his BBC interview: "Anyone who seriously considers himself a businessman in today's modern world must at least think like a Jew." Though even the quote, I discover, was lifted from William Rees-Mogg in his book *The Reigning Error: The Crisis of World Inflation*.

Noticeably, I take a good deal of poetic license in building my case. Nevertheless, I don't make it up and my licence remains one of life's luxuries that even a poor man can afford . . . .

Possibly only a poor man.

VI

On War

" WAR is the highest form of sabotage, the most atrocious form of sabotage. Usurers provoke wars to impose monopolies in their interest, so that they can get the world by the throat. Usurers provoke wars to create debts, so that they can extort the interest and rake in the profits resulting from changes in the values of the monetary units." ("The Enemy Is Ignorance," 1944, E. Pound)

Here, Pound gives the reason for creating wars, those pernicious motives lurking behind the scenes. Wars, as he had told us earlier on, "are created in succession," becoming the means from which usurers—financiers, monopolists and arms merchants—gain benefit. In the days of ole,' lords of war gained wealth *by* war, or lost it, in the course of battle, as opposed to those who introduced that new spirit of enterprise that gained wealth *from* or out of war. This is an axiom of Werner Sombart found in his book *The Jews and Modern Capitalism* (1915), who introduced the grammatical use of precise preposition to help us recognize that spirit which found a way to benefit without having to fight.

In 1862, the Hazard Circular, printed in the U.S. said: "The great debt that [our friends the] capitalists [of Europe] will see to it is made out of the war must be used to control the volume of money... It will not do to allow the greenback, as it is called, to circulate... for we cannot *control* them." (My italics.)

This was only one of the battles Lincoln lost, as he was forced to his knees by the powerful banking houses from whom he needed money to fight a war. His attempt to print the Union's own legal tender, *i.e.* greenbacks, was one way he sought to avoid taking it from the banks at thirty-four percent interest. The Union's own eventually went under, as did Lincoln himself,*"with the waiting depot, the arriving coffin and the sombre/ faces/"* (Whitman's "When Lilacs Last in the Dooryard Bloom'd"). The passing of Lincoln cleared the way for the National Banking Act. This Act, which gave unprecedented control of currency and credit to private (often foreign) banking interests, was the brainchild of those very Rothschilds, who, if Jonathan Swift had invented them, could not have played the part more aptly. The result of Lincoln's failure, in so much as he, like the Emperor Shun, felt responsible, was expressed in Lincoln's own words, "a black spot on the soul of the Nation [its National Debt]," as Dante himself might have put it.

The issue of the American Civil War and what it was fought over has never been made clear by even a few historians. Pound insists that it was the two-hundred-million-dollar debt owed by the South (1800s!) to New York banks that was squeezing the southerners so badly that secession was seen as the only way out. The blood-letting that ensued was one of the worst the world has ever seen, and when the cannon smoke finally cleared there appears a single nemesis with stained hands.

This period of U.S. history can be seen as the aftermath of the earlier American Conflict, the battle with England, from which Pound's Homeric Heroes, Thomas Jefferson and John Adams, emerge. By reversing the navigational course from the 1860s and what Pound cited as the point of "decline of American Civilization" back to the hard-fought battles of independence, we can enter by way of the Cantos.

Thomas Jefferson makes his appearance in Canto XXI, via a written request

"Could you", wrote Mr. Jefferson,
"Find me a gardener
Who can play the french horn?

Jefferson informs us that:

> The bounds of American fortune
> Will not admit the indulgence of a domestic band of
> Musicians, [...]

and therefore he expresses his hopes that by way of domestic servants in his employ,

> A gardener, a weaver, a cabinet-maker, and a stone-cutter,

he can create a small ensemble. As a member of the Continental Congress (1775), U.S. Minister to France, (1785-98), Secretary of State (1790-93), and Vice President (1797-1801) then as the third U.S. President (1801-1809), he shows himself, like Sigismundo in Renaissance Italy, to be a beneficent ruler for whom culture and art are for people of all walks of life. Later in Canto XXI, Jefferson arranges for Tom Paine, the political philosopher, to obtain passage to America. This was in 1801, but as an example stands with those other men already *assembled* and present in the Cantos:

> Patrick Henry, Frank Lee and your father,
> Henry Lee

who join Jefferson and John Adams to make a stand and prepare with intelligence to fight the battle yet un-won well after '76. The dating starts in 1773, prior to the revolt and proceeds on past the third president.

The ten Cantos XXXI-XLI, together with the Fifth Decade of Cantos (XLII-LI) and including Cantos LII-LXXI, contain extensive historical material on all these men, adding Van Buren and Franklin to the expanding orchestration Pound has already given us. England had *sold itself* to the Bank of England (1694), so it must be clear that, while unjust parliamentary laws imposed on the colonies were political issues, the issue was purely an economic one. The early American ambassadors who went to France in order to seek financing for The Revolution draw one in closer to realize that the hegemony of Banking houses was well established and in place at that time. In Canto XXXIV we find a conversation between the French ambassador, Armand Augustin Louis and John Quincy Adams, explaining that France will make peace with both England and America and normalize conditions for trade. Also in XXXIV, J.Q.A. on May 1815 meets with Sir James Mackintosh in London and tells him

Did not believe Dr Franklin or Washington
Had wanted the revolution . . . .

Far too much of this history has been glossed over with Tea Party stories and a disregard for details. Anybody having been schooled in either America or

England concerning this vital period hardly knows a damn thing.

Hearing again from John Quincy Adams, 1819:

> Banks breaking all over the country,
> Some in a sneaking, some in an impertinent manner...
> prostrate every principle of economy.
>
> Canto XXXIV

By 1841, Martin Van Buren, on the verge of his seventy-fourth birthday, with hands shaking and still working ten hours a day, has told us:

> The world, the flesh, the devils in hell are
> Against any man who now in the North American Union
> shall dare to join the standard of Almighty God to
> Put down the African slave trade ...
>
> Canto XXXIV

brings into focus another monumental economic factor within the overall issue. Adams reflects:

> Paper currency....reductions of fictitious capital....
> Accumulation of debts as long as credit can be strained....
>
> Canto XXXIV

Nearly any reference can rush into a slip-stream that lands us down river, 1860s, (or even 1933). Therefore, I need to keep paddling back to point out other references in mind. In Canto XLI, circa 1796, we have a letter from T. J. to Colonel James Monroe (a future president) who was then U.S. Ambassador to France.

> Public debt increasing at about one million a year
> You will see by Gallatin's speeches....
> Saddled by bank, led by a bridle
>
> Canto XLI

The actual letter by Jefferson is no less blunt. "You will see further, that we are completely saddled and bridled, and that the bank is so firmly mounted on us that we must go where they will guide." By Canto XLVI, both Jefferson and Van Buren are still resisting.

> Bank creates it ex nihil. Creates it to meet a need,
> Hic est hyper-usura. Mr. Jefferson met it:
> No man hath natural right to exercise profession
> of lender, save him who hath it to lend.

In Canto XLVIII, Pound states his belief that Martin Van Buren's Autobiography was buried for more than fifty years. John Adams exclaims in seeming frustration, 'deface and obliterate'

as Marx makes an appearance followed by a show from
Bismarck, who

    blamed american civil war on the jews;
    particularly on the Rothschild
    one of whom remarked to Disraeli
    that nations were fools to pay rent for their credit

    In Canto LII, Pound's tone and temper has
manifestly changed. He quotes an essay by Benjamin
Franklin (thought at the time to be authentic though
believed now by some not to be). I am fortunate to have a
copy of the item, and am in no position to doubt it.

    Remarked Ben: better keep out the jews
       or yr/ grand children will curse you
    jews, real jews, chazims, and *neschek*
    also super-neschek or the international racket
    specialité of the Stinkschuld
       bomb-proof under their house in Paris
    where they cd/ store aht voiks
       fat slug with three body-guards

soiling our sea front with a pot bellied yacht in the offing,
governments full of their gun-swine, bankbuzzards,
poppinjays.

Canto LII

[note: the word *neschek*, used above, being Hebrew for usury, and condemned by the law of Moses.]

It could be said more accurately that Pound is in a bad temper here. A few lines that immediately precede the Franklin bit are essential to keep in focus what the poet is revealing:

Stinkschuld's sin drawing vengeance, poor yitts paying for
Stinkschuld
paying for a few big jews' vendetta on goyim

Canto LII

However misspelled, the Rothschild name within the Cantos is the personification of usurers, and no matter how much historical documentation remains available to support Pound's choice, the true power of the poem is in the meanings purported to us. There had been, and still is, a privileged group of usurers whose effect on the world continues to devastate all natural life. Many of them, though not all, were and still are identifiable as jews. It is entirely possible to view the well-documented historical evidence that exists, from the time of Moses to the present, in an unemotional and scholarly manner. Any attempt to censor the poet (or any other person who is seriously examining this material) can be nothing less than the *covering-up* of the truth so as to allow the crime to continue.

It could become disorientating for the less-than-sturdy sea-legs of any navigator (of history) when trying to keep sight of the single thread that connects these events *Americana*. Back in the small New England town where I grew up, we'd get these flat stones and sling 'em side-arm across any of the many lakes and ponds we have around there. Three skips before *plunk* was good. I'll give it a try. (I) French/Indian War and the fight for the control of the colonial investments with the Brits. (II) The Revolutionary War fought against the British whigs and loyalists to the Crown by the Independentalists—who made arrangements to secure loans from France. (III) The years 1798-1800 and the end of the Adams presidency with Alexander Hamilton intriguing for a war with France. Hamilton still had a *whig* in his closet and his hand in the U.S. Treasury. Tom Jefferson who wanted no war, distrusted Hamilton, and did what he could to block him from becoming the next Secretary of War, *plunk*.

Hamilton no command,
too much intrigue. McHenry was Secretary for War, in 98

Canto LXX

McHenry, we learn, was later removed by John Adams who discovered he was working behind the scene with Hamilton. Hamilton, an early American traitor in Pound's view, was moving towards the *private sale* of the States to the First National Bank. It would take President Andrew Jackson, seventh in line (1828-1836), to block the re-issuing of the second Charter for the bank. Jackson is well known for being discredited and slandered in school books.

Back in 1808 and John Adams is out of the presidency, but still very much involved.

From England greater injuries
than from France,
I am for fighting whichever forces us first into a war.
depreciated by the swindling banks, a multitude
of such swindling banks have ruin'd our medium

Canto LXXI

This passage was Pound's paraphrase of an Adams letter which gives details of the banks' over-production of *baseless* paper that caused the price of labor, land, produce, and manufactured goods to be "doubled, tripled and quadrupled," while people's power to purchase fell far below what was needed.

Having gone up and down the river between the end of the eighteenth and first half of the nineteenth centuries, we arrive well within ear-shot of the American Civil War. The destruction of one war, the American Bankers' War (1861-65), echoes in our ear. In the 1920s, having moved from London to Paris, and after the senseless slaughter of the Great War, the poet wrote of the preconditions that lead up to all wars.

I o venni in luogo d'ogni luce muto;

Canto XIV

["I came to a place mute of all light."]

Pound intended these lines to reflect his mood on the London of his day, but they may serve well again. To complete the knot, through which the rope passes, I would conclude with the following: The American Continental War was lost by North 'n' South, black and white. This is the turning point of the Decline. Well before that point, wherever exactly it was, the stage had long since been set for a TRAGEDY. The die was cast for Pound's heroes as it was for Homer's.

IN 1944, Pound wrote of "AMERICA AND THE SECOND WORLD WAR," in an essay of the same name. Stating his case, he directs us to the causes of one war in order that we understand "the cause or causes of several—perhaps of all." "School-books," we are told, "do not disclose the inner workings of banks. The *mystery* of economics has been more jealously guarded than were ever the mysteries of Eleusis." Speaking of the Second War, Pound says, "that it was a secular war between usurers and peasants, between usurocracy and whomever does an honest day's work with his brain or hands."

Only one authentic historian has powerfully emerged to stand against the dominance of the Frankfurt School which arose in 1950 to establish a locked-in dialectic that at the end of the day provided the necessary debate that has sanctioned a structuralist world model sustained by usury. This man is Ernst Nolte. When Mr. Nolte's monumental study, *The European Civil War 1917-1945*, appeared, after the breakdown of the Cold War façade, a great break-through took place. Nolte applied the classical greek method used by the historian Thucydides, who having failed to make sense of the two great wars that destroyed Greece, recognized significant patterns which revealed that the two wars were in fact one. The essential kernel that we get from the great

German historian is that events from 1917-1945 represented one continuous struggle between two forces: National Socialism and International Socialism.

The victory of the Internationalists in 1945 was synonymous with the victory of Bolshevism. The two then became debate partners while the latter emerged in the 1960s as the topic of choice in every Western University from Paris to Berkeley. This *rhymes* with what Pound had said earlier about liberals and Bolsheviks being in complete accord. The autonomy of "the nation" was lost in '45, while the multi-nationals (and their Eastern-block-controlled conglomerate cousins) rose up. Likewise, any recent leader who rejected the world banking oligarchy and attempted to re-establish money on stable values (rice, for example, in Southeast Asia) has been ruthlessly branded as a brutal sub-human.

Harmonizing with the chord of multi-nationals during the post-war boom that saw the rise of America as a super power in the 50s and sixties, I propose descending the scale into the *muted domain*. Furtive voices start to become audible. John Pierpont Morgan (1837-1913), the American banker and financier whose company made a fortune out of the First World War by selling arms and credit to the European allies, is recognized. J. P. himself started out running guns for big profits during the Civil War. His dealings involved illegal practices with serious charges brought against him but from under which he eventually slipped out. Canto XL reveals that Morgan sold a debt (unpaid for rifles he got cheap) from one branch of the Federal Government to another department of the government.

> As to the government's arms: they were bought by
> one government office before they had been sold
> (as condemned) by another ditto (i.e. government office)
> passing through a species of profit sieve.
>
> Canto XL

Morgan's economic preference would be questioned again in 1913, but emerged unhurt by the investigation conducted by the House Committee on Banking and Currency.

Descending yet lower, with obvious trepidation, we approach the Eighth Circle, guarded by the three-headed Geryon. This is home to the rich and famous who have defrauded and sodomized the living creatures of earth. The stench! Presently we encounter Sir Basil Zaharoff, a European munitions magnate with major interest in oil, international banks and newspapers. The unconscionable Zaharoff is spotted, unpleasantly, sometimes under the name of Zenos Metevsky, 1850-1928.

Zaharoff started off selling arms for Nordenfeldt and Company around 1875 and eventually gained controlling shares, merged with Hiram MAXIM, who invented the machine gun, and in 1913, they joined Vickers-Armstrong to form the largest munitions company in Europe. With factories all over the continent special arrangements were made for them not to be bombed during the First War. The German firm, Krupp, another company controlled by Zaharoff, makes barbed wire for France and the Schneider-Creusot factory (in France) will not be hit. Turks use Vickers shells against Brits. Metevsky was a wizard at playing off two ends against the middle. He made money hand over fist, and even when he made enemies he was no less clever in his escapes. While under the name of Zacharias Basileos Zaharoff, Metevsky was imprisoned in Athens, this time getting caught in one of his unethical plans. An escape attempt is made by a man believed to be Zaharoff, who gets shot by the warden, then carried off and buried. Zaharoff was able to sit in a café and watch the whole affair.

> And Metevsky died and was buried, *i.e.* officially,
> And sat in the Yeiner Kafé watching the funeral.
> About ten years after this incident,
> He owned a fair chunk of Humbers.
>   "Peace! Pieyce!!" said Mr. Giddings,
> "Uni-ver-sal? Not while yew got tew billions ov money,"
> Said Mr. Giddings, "invested in the man-u-facture
> "Of war machinery. [...]
>   Canto XVIII

Metevsky, not content to work only the European market, makes a big arms deal with two South American belligerents, Bolivia and Paraguay.

AN' that year Metevsky went over to America del Sud

Canto XXXVIII

Vickers, the huge ARMS manufacturer, is now in Metevsky's control and reads Akers in the continuing Canto. Just before Metevsky cuts the deal, Pound inserts a short biographical note about Sir Basil, or rather about his mistress, Lucrezia who was married to the heir of the Duke of Ferrara. *Dear* Lucrezia, who was also the daughter of Pope Alexander VI, had three children and five abortions, dying during the fifth. The aborted birth having something to do with her lover, Metevsky. The short passage, inserted to emphasize, will rhyme with what Pound would write in Canto XLV:

Usura slayeth the child in the womb

The link is between the ARMS INDUSTRY and usury with both being

CONTRA NATURAM

Canto XLV

The South American deal goes down with Sir Basil
Zaharoff cutting the deck.

Don't buy until you get ours.

And he went over the border

and he said to the other side:

The *other* side has more munitions. Don't buy

until you can get ours.

And Akers made a large profit and imported gold into England

Canto XXXVIII

The nineteen-twenties are drawing to a close and
war is on the rise. The stock market too has been going
through the roof and is about to *crash* into the cellar.
Upon entering the 1930s, while the world is preparing for
another Great War, Pound began what could well be
claimed as the most powerful and fecund decades of his
career. The 1940s brought America "officially" into war;
as one Congressman exclaimed, "War is the only way
out," "to signify that Roosevelt had made such a mess
out of things..." (*An Introduction to the Economic Nature of
the United States*, 1944.)

Tempus tacendi, tempus loquendi

Canto LXXIV

["A time to speak, a time to be silent."]

Never inside the country to raise the standard of living
but always abroad to increase the profits of usurers,
    dixit Lenin,
        and gun sales lead to more gun sales
          they do not clutter the market for gunnery
there is no saturation
                      Canto LXXIV

"All this," we are told in Pound's *Guide to Kulchur*, from the chapter "Sophist," "is still blank in our histories. "Wars are paid for by depreciation of currency," wars are paid for in blood and carnage, indiscriminate murder is respectable, discriminate murder is criminal, and so forth, *so weiter, etcetera*." A *coup d'état* is prompted by foreign (insider) interests, followed by currency devaluation. The "world market price" of a targeted country's prime export suddenly drops. Cities are devastated under guise of Allied Forces routing an enemy, and they leave their calling card.

```
WE DO REBUILDING
AND CONSTRUCTION

Secretary of State
[part-time executive of Becktel Corp]

Call for (Un)reasonable rates.
```

This chapter On War can more appropriately represent the poet's all-out War On usury. The fact that he took this on and made it his fight distinguishes him as one of the most heroic men of the twentieth century. *The Cantos* are as much a great telling of history, seen from the perspicacious prow of the poet's craft, as they are one man's passionate response to the Divine.

> Oh you who believe, fear God
> > and give up what remains of
> > your demand for usury, if you
> > are indeed believers.

> If you do not, take notice
> of War from God and His
> Messenger.

Qur'an: 2.275/279

VII

Light Verse

"THIS book is not written for the over-fed," reads the opening line in Pound's prologue to the *Guide to Kulchur*, first printed in 1938. Thereby, Pound indicates that his students must possess a certain *leanness* that will affect their *need*. He did not, however, write for the starving, but that some able-bodied men and women should gain sufficient knowledge to create a system of governance and a healthy means of exchange that could safeguard against infamy. Pound's *Guide* is to be of help to young students and also the not-so-young "who want to know more at the age of fifty than I know today." When a people lose their curiosity they begin to sink.

Pound took unreasonable risks in what he wrote, yet in his own view he would have been "a cad not to." His freedom cost him. At no time did he cling to a safe harbor tied to an academic post. Nor did he recline in the comfortable salons of an art world that pandered to the supermarket tastes of modern publishing houses. Pound used a statement of one of his talented contemporaries, the sculptor Jacob Epstein, that refuted unemployment by saying, "I make my own work." Pound liked this comment and knew it could work for a few thousand artists and creative types including himself. Nevertheless, he was never (except possibly in 1908 when he arrived in England as the outrageous young contender) interested solely in an élite circle of people being able to survive a corrupt world. He was aware of the millions while working amongst a select body. Neither did he wallow in an egocentric marsh of universal empathy like his fellow American bard of the previous century. Whitman did, to his credit, write a dozen or so beautiful lines of *vers libre* in the English language. Pound did, however, much more than Whitman ever did, live his life surrounded by people whom he loved and who loved him. There were two great women, Dorothy and Olga, and I'd add a third, his gifted daughter, Mary. There were his friends, fellow artists, as well as his parents, particularly his father, Homer. Pound was at the center of all these people like the point of a huge VORTEX. His search for knowledge was never divorced from action: The Unwobbling Pivot, from the Master Kung. Many would argue that in the end he was more shattered than whole.

M'amour, m'amour
　　what do I love and
　　　where are you?
That I lost my center
　　fighting the world.
　　The dreams clash
　　　and are shattered —
and that I tried to make a paradiso
　　　　terrestre

　　　　　from Notes for Canto CXVII

While the entire industrialized world was hurtling
into the powerful sweep of the Maelström that
characterized the 1950s and '60s, bringing to an end many
cultural traditions that had held peoples' lives together
with meaning, Pound was completing his elliptic tracing
back to Koung-fu-Tseu and an up-to-date understanding
of economics. "When one knows enough, one can find
wisdom in the Four Classics" [the three books of
Confucius and one of Mencius]. "When one does not
know enough one's eye passes over the page without
seeing it." This paradise n'est pas artificiel. The canopy of
stars could be seen on a clear night and were painted on
the blue dome of Galla Placidia's mausoleum, thanks to
Sigismundo of Rimini. JUST rulers are preservers. The

Chinese sage/kings blend wisdom and strength and
thereby see to it that the granaries are maintained and the
channels of distribution unobstructed. Without love of
knowledge, good men become bad ones.

> You have heard the six words, and the six
> becloudings? There is the love of being benevolent,
> without the love of learning, the beclouding here
> leads to foolish simplicity. The love of knowing
> without love of learning, whereof the beclouding
> brings dissipation of mind. Of being sincere without
> the love of learning, here the beclouding causes
> disregard of the consequence. Of straight-
> forwardness without the love of learning, whereof
> the beclouding leadeth to rudeness. Of boldness,
> without the love of learning, whereof the
> beclouding brings insubordination. The love of
> firmness without the love of learning, whereof the
> beclouding conduces to extravagant conduct.

In 1933, Benito Mussolini opposed the consortium of
potbellies, "hoggers of harvest," that had the country in
financial ruin. This consortium was one of leading
bankers, and, together with the money-drain of the Pope,
the marshes could not be drained and put to good civic
use for people's needs.

"Where the Pope goes is lack of money
Because of the mass of clerics
   who bring cheques for the banks to cash,

Canto XLI

Most will not make a connection between Confucius
and the Italian dictator, but there was a time, said a
dignified old waiter in Rapallo, that "we were all
fascists." I knew that the rich tourists didn't like that kind
of talk by the locals. The waiter had to be very discreet.
The illustrious corpses of political power occupy the
janitor's quarters and are mistaken for the masters of the
house. The real business goes on upstairs and no one
knows their names. In his day, Ezra Pound named names
and they sure as hell didn't like it. Free elections with the
candidates provided by CENTRAL CASTING, who know
the mood of the nation. The current world leadership is
bankrupt.

Democracies electing their sewage
till there is no clear thought about holiness
a dung flow from 1913
and, in this, their kikery functioned, Marx, Freud
   and the american beaneries
Filth under Filth,

Cantos XCI

Contrasting those dark passages are lines from the same canto

> That the sun's silk
>
> hsien   顯   tensile
>
> be clear

Canto XCI

The ideogram for *hsien*, a tensile light, is enormously important to the understanding of Pound. It is the light that descends upon man, Dante's Divine Intellect. It appears again in Canto XCVIII descriptively:

> by the silk cords of the sunlight,
> Chords of the sunlight (*Pitagora*)
>   non si disuna (xiii)

The third line, from above, *non si disuna*, is taken from Dante's Paradiso and reads: "not disunited" (from its Lucent Source). Without giving all of the occurrences of this particular light, it can be said that it is one that inspires intelligent discrimination, recognition and knowledge of things defined. The Neoplatonists come into it. The pre-Socratic philosophers and Ibn Rushd and

Ibn Sina and Al-Kindi come into it. The neo-Confucian sages, also, of course, are present. These are the men of great intellect within *The Cantos* and, like the men who RULED by Justice, they too occupy a special standing in the great poem.

> by the silk cords of the sunlight
> > non disunia,

> > > Canto XCIX

The "silky light" comes down pure, spun from a legend of the cocoons tucked up in an old woman's apron. Immaculata.

> There are six rites for festival
> > and 7 instructions
> that all converge as the root tun^1 pen^3

> [tun = "root," pen = "to urge," hence, Pound's converge]

> the root veneration (from Mohamed no popery)
> To discriminate things
> > shih$^{2\text{-}5}$ solid

> > > Canto XCIX

The teaching revealed to Mohamed [sic]is *no popery* and confirms Pound's understanding of clear proofs or signs ("ayats"). This "discriminating" comes into medieval thought via Averroes (Ibn Rushd) and according to Carroll F. Terell's *Companion to the Cantos of Ezra Pound*, "was advanced by Siger de Brabant in the thirteenth century." Siger is given a place of eternal light in Dante's Paradiso [Par. X136], while the papal position is in contentious opposition to his understanding. In Canto iv of Dante's *Inferno*, Plato, Aristotle, Zeno, Ibn Sina and Ibn Rushd are all honored, along with a few other notable Greek philosophers. None of them having been baptized, they were relegated to reside in Limbo. Dante, understandably, had a certain bias, while, at the same time, he did not fail to recognize the illuminated. According to the historian Singleton, Siger "was no doubt one of those at whom in 1270, a general condemnation of Averroism was aimed." The consensus among Pound scholars has been that the early Christian thinkers Pound celebrates are closer to the Islamic tradition expressed by Ibn Rushd (Averroes) and Ibn Sina (Avicenna) than the latter day Church. Regarding this affinity, Terrell says: "The issue is by no means a minor one in Pound's religion. Faith based on a continuous denial of reason and of solid objective evidence is destructive both to the religious sect that requires it and the adherents of such a sect [religion]: such rhetorical dogma is 'popery.' "

From the well-planned gardens of Confucian China, through the date groves of Madinah and on into Andalucía (Averroes was born in Córdoba), a well-trodden path can be found.

The scene shifts. Once more the darkness moves in, penumbrae move about casting in and out of sight the overgrown path. In "Addendum for C," written about the same time as Cantos XLV and LI, in 1941, Pound brings to bare the evil of usury, translated as *neschek* in Hebrew and as Τόχοζ in the Greek with *hic mali medium est* ("here is the center of evil.") Appears too Fafnir from Wagner's Ring, the giant *contractor* who turned into a dragon to protect what he had stolen from his brother, noticeably contrasting with Kung's *"brotherly deference"* (Canto XIII).

The Evil is Usury, *neschek*
the serpent
neschek whose name is known, the defiler,
beyond race and against race
the defiler
Τόχοζ hic mali medium est
Here is the core of evil, the burning hell without let-up,
The canker corrupting all things, Fafnir the worm,
Syphilis of the State, of all kingdoms,

Addendum for C

With continual difficulty, Pound must find his way back,

> over the shambles,
> and some climbing
> before the take off,
> to "see again,"
> the verb is "see" not "walk on"
> i.e. it coheres all right
> even if my notes do not cohere.

Canto CXVI

Here the student needs to salute his teacher and *walk on*, and, with the support of companions, to "make it new." The poet's accomplishment is in what he saw and how he told the tale.

But to affirm the gold thread in the pattern

Canto CXVI

As we approach the final lines of the Cantos, we are aware of having travelled with an intrepid voyager, possessed of keen intelligence and wonderful wit. "To have begun with a swollen head and ended with swollen feet."

A little light, like a rushlight
    to lead back to splendour.

                    Canto CXVI

The *light imagery* of the Cantos is its connection to
the Sublime.

    In the light of light is the *virtù*
      "sunt lumina" said Erigena Scotus

                    Canto LXXIV

[In the light of light is the "creative power" (from Virgil);
"*sunt lumina*" is from a line in the book *De Divisione
Naturae* by Johannes Scotus Erigena, which was
condemned by Pope Honorius III (1225). "All things that
'are lights.'"]
    An élite is distinguished by those who, while
seeking that "blindn light," recognized that they are
charged in this world with establishing "order" and
"brotherly deference." Hence, no Taozers mooching
about, begging for alms to build gold palaces for "the
Bhud." And since the young Sidhartha rejected all that
and set out to travel, what makes 'em think he would
want the place? "No monkery," said the Prophet.
Confucius, too, *weren't no taozer*, while he was on the *tao*

(path) of the ancients. Pound translated the character for
tao as *process* and, while Kenner suggests that E. P. "may
have supposed for a long time that Kung's *tao* and Lao
Tzu's were different words," (*The Pound Era*), it is not
likely Pound missed the active principle in its meaning.
Two things that appear opposite have to be held in the
mind at the same time.

At the end of his life the American poet believed he
didn't know much. He was freed of a great illusion.

> Do not move
>> Let the wind speak
>>> that is paradise.

Notes and Fragments

Postface

There was a great man of the eighteenth century by
the name of Mawlay al-Arabi ad-Darqawi who said an
extraordinary thing. This man, who is called Shaykh ad-
Darqawi, said about the path (the Way) of knowledge that
it lies through the wheat-field. He meant by this that the
way (the *tao*) is service: serving the people. In this we can
hear the words of the ancient Chinese sages who, while
occupied with the rectification and purification of their
hearts, simultaneously were engaged in establishing
justice, maintaining the granaries, facilitating irrigation
and cultivation of the land and protecting the channels of
distribution and commerce. We can, likewise, recognize
that this tao, what Pound translated as process, is not
other than *The Tao* of Lao-Tzu. Unlike the passive inter-
pretation that led to a spiritual decadence, Kung-futz-æ
and the rulers who followed him in his mobilized
understanding were concerned with "order" and
"brotherly deference." They were preservers of the forms
of courtesy and noble character through the remembrance

of the still more ancient odes and rituals. It is precisely by turning away from the self and its arena of worldly ambition together with turning towards the needs of others and accepting (and taking on) authority that real leadership comes about.

Living today there is a teacher who is the inheritor of this knowledge and is the heir of Shaykh ad-Darqawi. Having had the benefit and privilege of sitting in his company I will relate what he explained as a further clarification of the line by the Master ad-Darqawi: "The way leads through the wheat-fields." Paraphrasing from memory, the understanding I gathered was this:

Those people who seek that knowledge which leads on to perfection of Absolute Being in which all existence other than the Existent is annihilated are like the growing field of wheat. These people, bowing and bending in the wind, rising up and standing golden-brown in the summer's sun are the shafts that will make the autumn's harvest.

Now this wheat must be cut, threshed and the chaff separated, then ground under the weight of enormous stones to be turned into flour. This flour must be salted and yeasted, allowed to rise, then punched down to rise again. The dough is then molded and shaped and put into tremendous ovens and baked under a great heat. What comes out is bread that now must be sliced and given to people to eat.

The kernel of this metaphor is that those people of knowledge are the leaders: they establish governance based on justice; they clean up and purify the trading markets, I mean, by prohibiting usury, fraud and any form of monopoly. Such a people, no longer driven by ambition and pride, no longer imagining that they are the creators of their actions, are set free. This is the condition of those that rule and are the caretakers of traditions and the preservers of language.

Ezra Pound recognized the existence of this quality of being in the great Chinese sages and, to a somewhat more limited degree, in others of his heroes who appear in the Cantos. Pound recognized that refined intelligence, which he expressed through light imagery, that imbued the hearts of men of old who had set out to make a world that reflected Divine Intelligence. Moreover, he saw that usury, with its root being *avarice*, fed by a lust of pecuniary gain with complete disregard for consequences incurred by the rest of humanity, was the single most destructive and pernicious practice that put all the beauty of life in peril.

It cannot however be said that Pound possessed the science of how to *make* men and women who are able to change both themselves and the world around them. That is another matter. The fact that he was able to see some of the triumphant possibilities that belong to man, expressing their deepest nature, raises him up as a signpost on the roadside. Herein lies the epitaph of the poet.

The analogy of the wheat-field is drawn from a source that affirms a knowing of how to guide and instruct, through the steps of transformation, those people who desire it. This is the highest knowledge. Shaykh Abdalqadir al-Murabit, who encouraged me to write this book, is such a teacher. The knowledge that is gained, as I understand it, changes one's inwardness as well as how one lives. How we are in our homes, how we transact in the world, the money that we use, must all be different. The gold thread in the pattern goes on and on. We must realize our need and it must be great. Unable to accept being a slave to tyranny, man needs courage to change.

> Her name was Courage
> & is written Olga

> Fragment (1966)

This reference to Olga Rudge can be seen as a touching tribute to one of the two great women the poet lived with. More importantly it is proof of Pound's deep existential commitment to live in a fuller and more complete way. Pound's love and respect for Olga, which reminds one of D. H. Lawrence's lifetime's work to rediscover the true collaborative nature of man and woman, demonstrates that Pound had crossed the threshold of that great mystery. The wonderful discovery that Richard Wagner died while in the process of writing a major essay on the 'nature of woman,' draws us on to further knowledge.

What thou lovest well remains,
　　　　the rest is dross
What thou lov'st well shall not be reft from thee

Canto LXXXI

The *terra firma of our very existence is under seige.* How *we transact in our lives, what in Arabic is called deen,* must be freed from the impediments of ignorance and tyranny.

"I keep hearing lines from the Cantos."
"The man saw it all!" exclaimed my compañero as we sat in the Cypriot café accross from Kensington Gardens.
"Andiamo!"

Bibliography

Ackroyd, Peter. *Ezra Pound.* London: Thames and Hudson Ltd., 1980.

Alighieri, Dante. *The Vision.* Translated by Rev. H.F. Cary, A.M. London: James Finch and Co., Ltd., 1844.

Alighieri, Dante. *The Paradiso.* Translated by John Ciardi. A Mentor Book, New American Library, 1970.

Anas, Malik ibn. *Al-Muwatta.* Translated by Aisha A. Bewley. Granada: Madinah Press, 1989.

Bacigalupo, Massimo. *Ezra Pound—un Poeta a Rapallo.* Genova: Edizioni S. Marco dei Giustiniani, 1985.

Berry, Wendell. *Standing by Words.* San Francisco: Northpoint Press, 1983.

Berry, Wendell. *The Unsettling of America—Culture and Agriculture.* San Francisco: Sierra Club Books, 1977 & 1986.

Bush, Janet. *London Times.* 30 January, 1993.

Clark, Abdassamad. *Father Jeremiah O'Callaghan, 1780-1861.* (Unpublished essay, Dublin, Ireland.)

Cookson, William. *A Guide to the Cantos of Ezra Pound.* London & Sydney: Croom Helm Ltd., 1985.

Dallas, Ian. *The New Wagnerian.* Granada: Freiburg Books, Granada, 1990.

Dallas, Ian. *Oedipus and Dionysus.* Granada: Freiburg Books, 1991.

Davis, Earle. *Vision Fugitive.* University Press of Kansas, 1968.

Deathridge, J. and Dahlhaus, Carl. *The New Grove Wagner.* New York; London: W.W. Norton and Company, 1984.

Del Mar, Alexander. *History of Monetary Systems.* London: 1895.

Del Mar, Alexander. *History of Monetary Systems of England, Germany and France.* New York: Cambridge Encyclopaedia Company, 1903.

Del Mar, Alexander. *History of Money in Ancient Countries.* London: George Bell and Sons, 1885.

Del Mar, Alexander. *Money and Civilization.* London: George Bell and Sons, 1886.

Del Mar, Alexander. *Usury and the Jews.* San Francisco: I.N. Choynski, 1879.

Doolittle, Hilda. *Selected Poems of H.D.* New York: Grave Press, Inc.

Edwards, J. H. and Vasse, W. W. *Annotated Index to the Cantos.* Berkeley and Los Angeles: University of California Press, 1957.

Ellul, Jacques. *Propaganda.* New York: Vintage Books, 1973

Emery, Clark. *Ideas into Action.* Coral Gables, Florida: University of Miami Press, 1958.

Heymann, C. David. *Ezra Pound, The Last Rower* New York: Viking Press, 1976. Seaver Books edition, 1980.

Kenner, Hugh. *The Pound Era.* Berkeley and Los Angeles: University of California Press, 1971

Laughlin, James. *Pound As Wuz.* St. Paul, Minnesota: Graywolf Press, 1987.

Makin, Peter. *The Cantos of Ezra Pound.* London: Allen and Unwin, 1985. Johns Hopkins University Press edition, 1992.

Miller, James E. *The American Quest for a Supreme Fiction.* Chicago: University of Chicago Press, 1979.

Murabit, Shaykh Abdalqadir. *Sign of the Sword.* Norwich: Madinah Press, 1984.

Murabit, Shaykh Abdalqadir. *For the Coming Man.* Norwich: Murabitun Press, 1988.

Murabit, Shaykh Abdalqadir. *The Bankers War—1914-1919.* Norwich: Murabitun Press (Pamphlet Series), 1990.

Nietzsche, Friedrich. *The Works of Friedrich Nietzsche: The Genealogy of Morals.* London and Leipzig: T. Fisher Unwin, 1899.

Ovid. *Metamorphosis.* Translated by Mary M. Innes. London: Penguin Classics, 1955.

Postman, Neil. *Amusing Ourselves to Death.* London: Penguin Books, 1985.

Pound, Ezra. *ABC of Economics.* London: Faber and Faber, 1933.

Pound, Ezra. *The Cantos.* London: Faber and Faber, 1986.

Pound, Ezra. *Collected Early Poems.* New York: New Directions Books, 1982

Pound, Ezra. *The Guide to Kulchur.* London: Peter Owen, 1952.

Pound, Ezra. *Impact.* Chicago: Henry Regnery Company, 1960.

Pound, Ezra. *Gold and Work.* London: Peter Russell, 1951.

Pound, Ezra. *Literary Essays of Ezra Pound.* Edited by T. S. Eliot. London: Faber and Faber, 1954.

Pound, Ezra. *Selected Poems.* New York: New Directions Books, 1957.

Pound, Ezra. *Translations of Ezra Pound.* London: Faber and Faber, 1953.

Pound, Ezra. *A Visiting Card.* London: Peter Russell, 1952.

de Rachewiltz, Mary. *Ezra Pound: Father and Teacher: Discretions.* New York: New Directions Books, 1957.

Rees-Mogg, William. *The Reigning Error: The Crisis of World Inflation.* London: Hamish Hamilton, 1974.

Sombart, Werner. *The Jews and Modern Capitalism.* London, 1913. Burt Franklin Press (New York) edition, 1969.

Sombart, Werner, *The Bourgeois.* Translated by M. Epstein. London: T. Fisher Unwin, 1915.

Terrell, Carroll F. *A Companion to the Cantos of Ezra Pound.* Berkeley: University of California Press, 1980 (Volume I); 1984 (Volume II).

Theobald, John. *Ezra Pound: Letters.* Redding Ridge, Connecticut: Black Swan Books, 1984.

Vadillo, Umar. *The End of Economics.* Granada: Madinah Press, 1990

Vadillo, Umar. *Fatwa on Paper Money.* Granada: Madinah Press, 1991.

Vadillo, Umar. *The Workers Have Been Told a Lie About Their Own Situation.* Granada: Madinah Press Pamphlet Series, 1992.

Index

❧